Bound 1968

This book may be kept

FOURTEE

REALITY AND THE POET
IN SPANISH POETRY

REALITY AND THE POET
IN SPANISH POETRY

1561

BY

PEDRO SALINAS

Translated by
Edith Fishtine Helman

with an Introduction by
Jorge Guillén
Translated by Elias L. Rivers

BALTIMORE
THE JOHNS HOPKINS PRESS

Originally published, 1940

Johns Hopkins Paperbacks edition, 1966

To

ELEANOR LAURELLE TURNBULL

FOREWORD

Jorge Guillén writes poetry, and also analyzes it, with penetrating insight and formal precision; he incarnates in one person the twin gods of creation and criticism. His poetry ranges from the jubilant joy of *Cántico* to the anguished chords of *Clamor*. His criticism has illuminated aspects of Spanish literature from its beginnings to the present century. He is also a scholar and a teacher, a man of friends and grandchildren. Since retirement as Professor of Spanish at Wellesley College, he has given courses and lectures at various universities. And his work as a poet continues as he moves toward the definitive edition of his collected poems.

It seems most appropriate that the Turnbull lectures on Spanish poetry, given in 1937 by the late Pedro Salinas and first published in 1940, should now be published in a new edition with Jorge Guillén's Turnbull lecture of 1966 as an introduction. Close friends and leading members of a great generation of Spanish poets, Salinas of Madrid and Guillén of Valladolid meet and recognize each other once again in these pages.

1966   Elias L. Rivers

INTRODUCTION: PEDRO SALINAS

by Jorge Guillén

I

Pedro Salinas: 1891–1951. The sixty years of his life constituted one single line of development. Thirty years of preparation. Thirty years of production. After the withdrawn boy, the reserved adolescent, the poet who wrote little and published less, there appears—beginning in 1923, the date of his first book, *Presagios*—a man of great complexity, an active personality, reaching full maturity during his last years, the Baltimore decade. His roots belong to Spain, Castille, Madrid. It is not enough to place our poet within the Castilian tradition. He was a man deeply rooted in the Madrid where he was born. And his Madrid was the most authentic Madrid, that of the " barrios bajos," the old city. Let us imagine Pedro as a little boy on the Plaza de Santa Cruz (made famous in the novels of Galdós), which he observed—or contemplated—from a balcony. Later he was to move to the house, his mother's house, on San Pedro Street, near the Church of San Andrés. (On that street had lived, yes, *lived*—with all the reality of Galdós's great fictional imagination—Feijoo, the character in *Fortunata y Jacinta*.) Here, in Baltimore, the native of Madrid was homesick not only for his country, but for his city. That was why he read Arniches, and even Madrid's very modest poet López Silva (the same López Silva whom, on a certain unforgettable occasion, Unamuno compared with Theocritus, to our delight and to the dismay of a very academic professor). This note of local color has been preserved in one of the poet's brief plays, *La Estratosfera, Vinos y Cervezas.*

After childhood and adolescence in Madrid there comes a widening of horizons. These are his three years in Paris as *lecteur* at the Sorbonne, from 1914 to 1917. Here begins his apprenticeship as a college teacher. But in France he learned, most of all, about literature; he absorbed the tradition of Baudelairean poetry. Taking advantage of Adrienne Monnier's rental library, across the Rue de l'Odéon from Shakespeare and Company, he continued reading in great quantities, as he always had. But literature was not the whole story: it was during that period, in 1915, that he married Margarita Bonmatí, who further widened his horizons, introducing him first to Alicante, where he met Valéry Larbaud and became a friend of Gabriel Miró. And Alicante implies North Africa: his wife was born in Algiers. We must not forget the Mediterranean background of our traveler's life and work, and the Andalusia which enriched his experience. In 1918 he moved to Seville, where he was a professor at the University until 1928. I have never known a Castilian who was more enthusiastic about Andalusian cities and landscapes than was Salinas. In them he discovered very special qualities, aesthetic affinities. He especially liked

Seville, whose heart for him was the Alcázar and its gardens. Among the lesser cities he preferred Ecija, San Fernando, Ronda. The poet and the traveler took simultaneous delight in Andalusia. This leisurely process of appreciation, so contrary to today's usual haste, was one of our friend's primary characteristics.

Naturally Salinas divided his time between Seville and Madrid. While he was still quite young he had joined Enrique Díez Canedo's group, noted for its discretion, culture, and elegant simplicity. Literarily precocious, but because of his high standards not prolific, he was also in contact with the slightly younger group which began to emerge about 1920. That generation—for even then one spoke of " generations "—took shape quite spontaneously. Salinas was to be the oldest member of that band—not a " school "—consisting of Gerardo Diego, Dámaso Alonso, Federico García Lorca, Vicente Aleixandre, Rafael Alberti, Luis Cernuda, Emilio Prados, Manuel Altolaguirre, several others, and the present writer. All these poets were held together by friendship, breathed the same air. But each one, in keeping with the spirit of the time, or rather the several different spirits of the time, had his own voice, which could not be reduced to a common denominator. Thus Pedro Salinas, in his originality, was simultaneously aware of European symbolism, French *vers libre*, Juan Ramón Jiménez's " verso desnudo."

Meanwhile, the social activities of the writer and the teacher were growing; he showed signs, no longer of timidity, but—who would have expected it?—of ability as an organizer. From Seville he was officially transferred to Madrid. He worked for a while in the national Patronato de Turismo. He also worked in the Centro de Estudios Históricos, where he founded the review *Indice Literario* and directed courses for foreign students. Moreno Villa, a member of the Residencia de Estudiantes, bears witness: " I do not think that anyone else has ever directed these courses with such natural ease and dignity." As an organizer his most important undertaking was the International University of Santander. Salinas was the person who conceived of the idea and proposed the plan, which was developed with the advice and aid of distinguished supporters and colleagues. It was an organization, as Salinas explains, " based on the co-operation of Spanish and foreign universities, which brought together for a brief period of intense work teachers and students from all the regions of Spain and from foreign countries, in order to carry out a joint program of study. . . ." Salinas, as secretary general, was the chief director, the " Maese Pedro," of that magnificent show from 1933 to 1936.

The fatal date, 1936. There began the tragic interruption, which for many Spaniards was the definitive one of death. The interruption of many careers, which were either destroyed or transformed. What happened to the Spain which could have been at that time? What would Salinas have been if he had continued to develop in his own country? He, like so many intellectuals, was to leave Spain never to return, and as an exile was to live on, in spite of everything, faithful to his vocation. Thus his career was fulfilled, not frustrated. Salinas' years in America were his most fertile ones. With the support of this country's generous hospitality Salinas was able to be more truly himself than ever before. Baltimore was his first haven. Here he gave his first lectures: *Reality and the Poet in Spanish Poetry.* (They were translated and rearranged for publication by the outstanding Hispanist Edith Helman; today only a portion of the Spanish original survives.) After four academic years at Wellesley College, he returned to Baltimore, where he belonged to the faculty of The Johns Hopkins University from 1940 to the end of his life, 1951. These were very good years, with Spitzer, Singleton, Lancaster, Dumont, Coleman . . .

Salinas devoted himself with real love and enthusiasm to " explicating " Spanish literature. There was no other occupation more suited to his intelligence and his preparation. Salinas would go to class expecting to spend a delightful period simply because he gave himself joyfully to that period. The classroom door did not suggest self-sacrifice to him. " They require us," he would say, " to talk about literature. And in addition they pay us money?! " Seldom has any man achieved such a harmonious balance of poet, critic, and teacher. (A teacher-poet? This double role was common in his day. In the tradition of Fray Luis de León, Unamuno, Antonio Machado, as well as Carducci, Mallarmé, and many others, Salinas and other literary men of his generation were indeed teacher-poets.) Concerning the Salinas of Johns Hopkins no words are more fitting than those of Professor Gillet, in his *Hispanic Review* necrology: " Hundreds of his students and colleagues will cherish their remembrance of his lectures, or rather his intimate lessons, for he was a born teacher, minutely scrupulous in his preparation, a master of order and clarity, dramatic and persuasive in his evident eagerness to share his understanding."

In Baltimore Salinas' production became more complex and profound. America, without a doubt, favored his productivity. Or let us say, in addition, that Baltimore coincided with the writer's maturity. Salinas was experiencing intensely his own life and that of the period. He was passionately interested in the historic events of the 1940's: history narrated day after day by the newspapers, those indispensable texts. Our insatiable reader read the newspapers with an avidity which went beyond the mere purpose of gathering information. He was a man with a very lively sense of justice, and he frequently suffered, in his conscientious heart, as a humanitarian and a humanist. He had an unusual capacity for indignation, offset by a great sense of humor. The " modern world " made him indignant, and fascinated him; it also constantly entertained him. How well acquainted he was with the United States! For Salinas, who was so fond of toys, this extreme manifestation of the " modern world " resembled an enormous, wonderful plaything, a " toyland " created by a god, Walt Disney. Salinas observed it with a delight which was critical; but criticism is always a form of authentic interest.

His interest extended to the whole of America. Salinas traveled throughout Spanish America, and these trips, long in distances and short in time, caused him pleasures and emotions which were not those of the simple tourist. They stirred up his Spanish roots. Spain lives without America; but one cannot know what Spain is if one does not discover Spanish America for oneself. The three years that Salinas spent in Puerto Rico were very happy. He liked everything in that Garden of Eden: the sky, the soil, the climate, the people—and their way of talking. It is hard on a writer to write when he is not surrounded by his own language, words floating in the air that one breathes. Salinas enjoyed that atmosphere so much that it was at the University of Puerto Rico that he gave his talk entitled "Appreciation and Defense of Language." For him that island was always enclosed within parentheses of felicity, both prose and verse. It was then that he composed what is perhaps his most luminous and serene poetry. There were also a few visits to Europe. His belated contact with Italy thrilled our traveler, who was so sensitive to the plastic arts, to beautiful cities. One day, here in Baltimore, Salinas told me quite solemnly (and he was not one to abuse solemnity): "Italy is more beautiful than Spain." And then: "Italy is the most beautiful country in the world." Salinas' avidness had no limits.

But our life does have limits. At the beginning of 1951 Salinas began to complain of tiredness, of aches. He was the complaining type, but this time he had a real reason to complain. The inexorable illness moved rapidly. And so, prematurely, in the most productive period of his life, most unjustly and incongruously, as the result of a most uncertain chance—Where was the "seguro azar," the "certain chance" of his youth?—Pedro Salinas died in Boston in that year of 1951: on the fourth of December.

He had just celebrated his sixtieth birthday. There was no possible consolation. One is aware in such cases of an injustice which is not even intentional: the absurd is irresponsible. " I trust in you, certain chance fulfilled," had sung the poet. We do not trust in you, absurd chance unfulfilled.

II

How can one put into words the glimmering flash of humanity, the unfailing spark which existed only in that particular being? Always essentially reserved, even timid, he seemed at times oblivious to what never ceased to guide him: his vocation. Pedro Salinas was able to fuse into a single whole his life and his career, his vocation, his actions, and his written works. In a Spanish character portrait of the fifteenth century he would have been called an " hombre esencial." An essential man! But so sensitive that he hung in front of his listener a curtain glittering with witticisms, jokes, playfulness. The world proffers itself, and there are no vacations for Salinas the alert explorer, always gazing, reading, traveling. No masterpiece would ever keep him from stopping to observe the simplest note of delight that might present itself to him at any turning of the street. He displayed such ingenuity, such a surplus of talent, that some people, failing to understand, considered him to be a " domineering " personality. Not at all! There was no one, inside, behind the gleaming facetious surface, more unsure of himself. It is true that he had overcome his youthful timidity. But he never lost his faculty for feeling shy—and complaining. Very often he would protest without taking at all seriously his own objections and complaints. He was always very human.

Baltasar Gracián wrote a treatise, which has been lost, entitled *The Attentive Man.* I have never known anyone who deserved that epithet more than our friend. Salinas' attentiveness was constant, meticulous, quite variable, and he focused it on . . . what? Everything, for everything affected his sensibility with the illumination of understanding. He was a master of delight. For him great constructions and sublime aspects were not the only things that existed. There are also everyday things that are so exquisite that they seem insignificant, subtleties that one must define with great care, for they elude eloquence. And is not this the realm of our most fragile treasures? Salinas, who was well aware of the supreme heights, was also an indefatigable discoverer of nameless little Indies. Curiosity, playfulness, discrimination, helpfulness: many sources contributed to his vast powers of attentiveness. And, finally, what is friendship but attention? The enormously attentive Pedro Salinas was eminent in the arts of friendship: he had a deep feeling for it, and he sensitively cultivated it with constant attentions.

III

Always in the foreground, confronting the observer, the appreciator, the critic, there was the literature that he loved. There was always a deciphering, analyzing intelligence accompanied by a sensibility ever active in delight.

For the critic pays attention only to great texts, and criticism functions as an act of admiration. But the poem, the novel, the play are there, facing the reader, in space and time. Without a sense of history one does not see the work, not even in an immediate sense. There is no present without history, nor are there historical values unrelated to present values; there is a close connection between interest in the literature of the past, and participation in contemporary literature. According to T. S. Eliot, " If we have no living literature, we shall become more and more alienated from the literature of the past." The criticism of our teacher-poet was always as living as it was historical. An excellent example of this is his book on Manrique, the subtitle of which sums up the whole matter: *Jorge Manrique, or Tradition and Originality.* How can one be aware of the originality of Manrique's poetry without exploring the deep tradition implicit within it?

" In literary history," says Salinas, " tradition is the poet's natural habitat. He is born into it poetically, in it he finds air to breathe, and within its scope his creative destiny fulfills itself." He then adds: " Tradition is the fullest degree of freedom that the writer can have. . . . The artist who manages to master his tradition is freer because he knows more lines along which to explore." And this is the consequence: " It thus seems that it is the duty of every artist to try to attain an awareness of the tradition in all its plenitude, to survey the broadest horizons available for the experiments of the creative spirit." Note that this process leads to a new originality. " Today," concludes our critic, " we look upon poetic creation as a total process, including all the psychological powers of the individual; the poet puts himself into his poem along with everything that he bears within himself, and when he enters the deep galleries in which he seeks his poem, he does not leave outside a single faculty of his soul." In keeping with these principles, stanza by stanza Salinas develops his analysis, always making use of previous criticism. Since his Manrique study is written in the style of a literary essay, his erudition is absorbed into the body of the text, not scattered in footnotes. Any other approach would have conflicted with the critic's standards and the writer's good taste, which are of course different from those of the philologian. Who has ever reproached Eliot's critical essays for not being " scholarly "? In Salinas too the critic is inseparable from the poet, for knowing is inseparable from making. (Let us not forget Vico's theory, that the way to know a thing is to make it, and that " the true " is " the thing made," the deed itself: *verum ipsum factum.*)

This was Salinas' way of searching out the work's most essential characteristic, and " essence " means " unity." Our author writes concerning the principles which guided him in his book on Rubén Darío's poetry: " It seems to me that the most fruitful activity in studying a poet is to define his theme with scrupulous discrimination, separating it carefully from secondary themes or sub-themes." Thus one achieves " a vision of the true creator as a whole, undistorted by mutilations and imprecise focus." To define the content obliges one, then, to define the form, for there is no content except in every tone and shading that expresses it, and verse reveals what it does reveal by grace of its words . . . and of its rhythmic ordering. Theme, structure, unity: everything converges toward a certain conception of man, a certain feeling for the human condition. " In every novelist," Salinas believed, " there is a unique intellectual and emotional vision of mankind, a particular conception of human nature." And elsewhere he adds: " There is no poet of stature who does not try to solve the riddle of the universe." These views are perfectly summed up in Juan Marichal's phrase concerning " the driving force behind Pedro Salinas' critical interpretations: the attempt to make evident the human values in the authors and works of Spanish literature." Language at its highest level. Human and formal values are inseparable. Or, in Salinas' words, " the spirit in its letter."

It was natural for him to cultivate the essay as well. Salinas' essays are unlike those of either Unamuno or Ortega y Gasset. " The defender " is what he called himself as an essayist, always critical of the commonplaces of his day, always defending humanism in the best sense. Hence his tendency toward a profound sense of unity with his fellow man. No ivory tower. " The poem," according to the defender, " born in solitude, will later revert to everyone, will reach out to everyone as it becomes a unifying force among men, revealing to them their mutual sympathies, in sum, their community as human beings." Communication may be either private or public. Privately, Salinas greatly enjoyed epistolary communication. The future edition of his letters will be a significant collection.

It is no accident that among his essays on Cervantes there is one called " The Best Love Letter in Spanish Literature," which is the letter that Don Quixote wrote to Dulcinea. With the greatest pleasure he retells the story of that fictional communication: an exquisite arabesque. Excellent also is his little treatise on letter writing. In this genre, the essay, culminate his gifts as a conversationalist, curious about everything, responsive to everything, but here disciplined, while still very personal, by the written form. All of his essays are interesting. We must here draw attention at least to " The Literary Minority," " The New Illiterates," " The Powers of the Writer " (that is, of the modern writer, chiefly represented by Balzac).

Since Salinas was, as Dámaso Alonso has said, " the literary man with the greatest variety of facets and attitudes in contemporary Spain," he naturally experimented also with dramatic dialogue and with narrative. While still in Spain he had written a three-act play, *The Director*. During the forties, in addition to a long work called *Judith and the Tyrant*, he wrote twelve short comedies. For him they were " reality in fable form." Precisely: an action situated on a normal level, so to speak, rises little by little, leaving behind that first level, until it reaches the heights of fantasy. One of these little works, *The Price*, is subtitled *Fantasy in One Act*. That is what all these comedies are, and among them *The Saints* is outstanding: in the midst of the Spanish Civil War there suddenly occurs, with deeply moving subtlety, a miracle, a genuine Catholic " miracle." Salinas was writing for the stage and would naturally like to have had his plays put on, not just read. But being in a non-Spanish-speaking country was a disadvantage to the budding playwright. He needed to see his works on the stage; he realized that only in that way could he reach maturity in this genre. Exile is not an unmixed blessing, though it does less harm to the normal development of the novelist. In 1926 Salinas had already published an experiment in lyrical prose, *On the Eve of Joy*, in the subtle style of that decade. The perspective is broader and deeper in *The Incredible Bomb,* with anguished echoes of the period following the Second World War, and in the series of *novelle* entitled *The Impeccable Nude*, the best of which is the title story. (The author changed its original title, *The Work of God*, when he realized that it coincided with " Opus Dei," the name of a flourishing new religious order in Spain.) The circle of the compass could have been the emblematic symbol of Salinas' fertile multiplicity in prose, which was constantly expressing itself, in the most lively and varied way, as a secondary activity, subordinated to his daily task of teaching and to his primary commitment, poetry.

IV

His poetic work consists of nine books, which may be grouped into three periods. The early period, from 1923 to 1931, includes *Presagios, Seguro azar,* and *Fábula y signo.* The second period, strictly speaking, constitutes a cycle: from 1933 to 1938 his great theme develops in *La voz a ti debida, Razón de amor,* and finally, a volume as yet largely unpublished, *Largo lamento.* With this cycle our author's activity reaches its highest point. But this metaphor is not intended to reduce the early period to a mere preliminary tryout, nor the later poems to a mere epilogue. Salinas is Salinas throughout his entire career; each volume contributes to defining the whole, and the whole is the most important aspect of a great poet's work. So the three volumes of the forties are also essential: *El contemplado, Todo más claro*, and the posthumous *Confianza*. (This final collection had no name; its general title is taken from that of one of the poems and is appropriate to Salinas' final style.)

The beginnings were slow. The youthful apprentice made great demands upon himself. *Presagios (Presciences)*, a word which the poet told me occurred to him as he was walking through the Puerta del Sol in Madrid, a word here used in its etymological sense, this word reveals a soul. And soul, as has already been said, is the key term of that poetry, a soul always in contact with the Other and the others. Inner life alone? A soul turned in upon itself? Not at all. The spiritual quality which is so evident in the whole work does not imply any solipsism, not even within the cloistered walls which are sometimes raised by love. Salinas is always involved in relationships of love or friendship with things and people, always ready to discover in them their value, their transcendence, their inner meaning. This vital meaning is understood and felt only when it is well fixed and rooted in a concrete particular.

From *Presagios* to *Confianza (Confidence)* we find a voice that delicately but firmly intensifies more and more this bringing to life of the world. That it has a soul is not a legend or a false ornamentation, but the deepest truth. Great poetry does not deceive itself, much less tell lies. Our poet knew what he was saying: *Fábula y signo*. All of his poems, not merely those belonging to the volume with this title, move from the fable to the sign: bringing an object to life reveals its transcendent meaning. Salinas' theme is, then, the conversion of the outer world into its inner soul, by means of friendship and love. *Todo más claro*: everything brighter. In his preface to this volume Salinas explains: " Whether it follows Saint Francis or Baudelaire, the *Fioretti* or the *Fleurs du Mal*, every poem worthy of the name achieves illumination." A completely human illumination, of course, without mystical implications. A " passion d'absolu " has been seen in Salinas by Elsa Dehennin, the intelligent and enthusiastic Hispanist of Belgium. The absolute is a very human goal. Salinas is always faithful to his vocation as a humanist.

How he gazed at his surroundings! His surroundings are loved and assimilated, above all, by his gaze. Vision is our poet's primary faculty. One desires what is real. And in order to convert it into spirit, one must go deep into matter. Not the orange, an easy solution, but its secret: the juice, an internal reality. One night in Amsterdam the traveler was attracted by some " green, red, blue, very rapid lights." " Do these lights belong to your soul, if I look at them? " the poet asks himself. Of course the external world is not self-sufficient, for in order to reach its fullness, it needs its complement. On a beautiful afternoon, blueness is not enough, " nor that singing repetition of the wave," nor the seashells as iridescent as clouds. All of those details are summed up, comprehended, and transcended by the spectator; it is he who brings the beautiful afternoon to its perfection. But this does not mean mere impressionism, a pleasant dissolving of the landscape into the sensations of an artist. The landscape is brought into relationship with an ideal significance. Nor is the sea during a summer's hour reduced to an " impression " of that hour. For him who contemplates it from this shore— " Orilla " is the title of a poem in *Seguro azar*—the sea throbs like an organic living animal, with a will of its own.

> *Si no fuera por la rosa*
> *frágil, de espuma, blanquísima,*
> *que él, a lo lejos, se inventa,*
> *¿quién me iba a decir a mí*
> *que se le movía el pecho*
> *de respirar, que está vivo,*
> *que tiene un ímpetu dentro,*
> *que quiere la tierra entera,*
> *azul, quieto mar de julio?*

> If it were not for the fragile
> rose of whitest foam
> invented by the distant sea,
> who would have thought
> that its breast moved
> with breathing, or that it's alive,
> that it's impetuous inside,
> that it wants the whole earth,
> the blue, quiet sea of July?

The words could not be more delicate, but they do not dissolve into a pictorial blob. The Mediterranean, viewed probably from a beach near Alicante, is transmuted, by grace of a metaphor, into a vision: the sea as a breast, the waves as the movement of one who breathes, breath as impetuosity or the will to power. And the foam, by an incidental metaphor, is converted into an " invented " rose: an ingenious stroke, offset by the very colloquial, and here very expressive, phrase, " ¿quién me iba a decir a mí? " From this shore, in sum, everything does look brighter, and its reality is made completely human: fable and sign. Does all this have anything at all to do with the " dehumanization " which was being talked about at the time?

The poet takes delight in the innumerable variety of things, and he does not exclude even the most recent things, from the automobile to the typewriter, those technical inventions which the " futurists " had already proclaimed. But innovations do not conceal the permanence of Nature. There is a " joyful knowledge "—that which is learned by contemplating natural life—which makes us able to endure the tribulations of historical life: Nature is our salvation. With what leisurely enjoyment he composes the poems of *El contemplado (The Contemplated Sea)* and *Confianza*! One must apply oneself lovingly to what one sees in order to reach what is not seen: the whole and its meaning. For, he tells us, " everything is on purpose, the world is headed somewhere." Everything is ordered and reaches a conclusion in meaningful action. That is how we perceive the total unity of the earth, which has, in fact, the perfection of the circle.

Un mundo rueda tranquilo.
¡Qué redondez tan perfecta!

A world turns peacefully.
What a perfect roundness!

Also, he tell us, " light is said to be round." This assertion
could not be proved by science. Nevertheless, from the
point of view of the soul's light, that other material light
does appear as something round and surrounding. What
re-creative power, piercing through everything with rays
of the human mind!

Pedro Salinas' poetry, we know, reached its highest
point with the theme of love. " Since Espronceda and
Bécquer," as I have said on another occasion, " since the
former's *Canto a Teresa* and the latter's *Rimas*, has there
been anything more important written in Spain than *La
voz a ti debida* and *Razón de amor?*" The lovers live by
themselves, seeking and finding one another, happy and
yet concerned, in their own insular world. That is the
way it always happens. Can there ever be lovers who are
not, or do not try to be, the sole inhabitants of an island
which is closed off from the rest of the world? For they
are a world in themselves. Salinas' love poetry does not
give us a strange, eccentric love, but one which is perfectly
normal, a love story which is fulfilled in a normal way.
The story itself amounts to no more than a series of situations involving sentiment, situations which never degen-
erate into sentimentalism, although they always retain
their warmth. These situations are developed and ana-
lyzed under a profound drive full of thought and feeling.

Thought, passion, tenderness, and sensuality are fully fused in this poetry which is made up exclusively of intense words. The voice owed to love, "la voz a ti debida," is impassioned throughout all its yearning researches. Where does so constant a yearning come from? There is no social conflict. Society then does not exist. Is there an internal conflict? No. The lover uses the love which he has attained as his point of departure and pursues the beloved, the most perfect beloved possible: the woman that love continues to discover and create, at the same time that it discovers and creates the lover. An ever new "I" eagerly pursues an ever new "you." I, you: that is all. The poet sums it up wittily: "It is the highest joy, simply to live in pronouns!" It is the "you and I" of all lovers which here acquires an extraordinary height and depth. Salinas pushes this basic situation to an extreme point of intensity and sublimation, without however destroying its naturalness. With regard to this we should recall Max Scheler, who has been referred to by several critics who have seen a relationship between his philosophy and Salinas' poetry. "Love only exists," we read in *Wesen und Formen der Sympathie*, "when in addition to the value already made real in love, there is the further movement or impulse toward further possible higher values. Precisely in the fact that love is motion in the direction of the highest level of value, precisely in this lies the creative significance of love." This is what Scheler says. And Salinas says to his beloved: "What I want to do is to draw out of you your best self." Thus the beloved, now nameless, is transformed into a You which hints at its own Beyond. Love must be sought and striven after, as it were, by fighting, and not against the beloved, but rather on her behalf, by striving in the direction of the best beloved possible.

Hence we find it incredible that Spitzer, the great philologian, Salinas' friend and colleague at this Johns Hopkins University, should have asserted: " It is a curious thing that even the beloved woman is negated by our poet; I am acquainted with no love poetry in which the two lovers are so completely reduced to the poet's own ego, in which the beloved woman lives only as a function of the man's mind and is no more than a phenomenon of his consciousness." What a monstrous conclusion! For once the great Spitzer made a mistake. There was every reason why Salinas, as he confessed to me here in Baltimore, should have been unable ever to read that essay, even though it is important in other respects. It is impossible that Salinas' love poems should have been merely " the metaphysical speculations of the poet by himself," that " the beloved is a purely abstract concept." Such are the extreme conclusions that a rigid intellectual formula can lead to, in this case the concept of " Spanish *conceptismo*."

As a matter of fact the poet pursues and encounters

> *esta corporeidad mortal y rosa*
> *donde el amor inventa su infinito.*
>
> This mortal, roselike corporeality
> where love invents its infinite.

An infinite that would be nothing at all without its adorable " locus ": " your sweet body in my thought." How could that thought ever have been born without the sweetness of that actual body? These images all tend to transport us to a planet which is governed by the law of gravitation.

> *Busca pesos,*
> *los más hondos, en ti, que ellos te arrastren*
> *a ese gran centro donde yo te espero.*
> *Amor total, quererse como masas.*

> Look for weights,
> the deepest ones, in yourself, and let them drag you
> down to that great center where I wait for you.
> Total love, the mutual attraction of masses.

The last line is quite clear, and its tone is emphatic. Totality, masses: total love, which extends from the presentiment to the fulfillment of love, almost from the very beginning, as is more solemnly declared in the longer poems of *Razón de amor (Love's Reason)*. Pedro Salinas already occupies a place which is very much his own, and very eminent, in the history of the love poetry of all times.

Love in its proper channels, friendship in all directions, writings that are complex and highly personal—and all in one of the most brilliant periods of Spanish literature, within that time of crisis which was the first half of the twentieth century. Here, in Baltimore, that great personality reached its full strength, always evoking loyal friendship and affection. Fortunately, he is still alive. In our hearts and in his books.

Spring of 1966

AUTHOR'S NOTE

The Johns Hopkins Press has kindly offered to publish these lectures which I had the honor to give at Johns Hopkins University, in 1937, on the invitation of the Turnbull Poetry Lectures Foundation. They are printed in this volume as they were given, without additions or changes.

It was always my intention to revise these lectures, to develop further some of the ideas and to add at least two more chapters, one on Gustavo Adolfo Bécquer, the great poet of romanticism, and another on Jorge Guillén, whose poetic treatment of reality, is, in my opinion, unique in Spanish poetry. Time and circumstances, however, bring them to the press in their primitive and imperfect state. They are offered to the reader with the true modesty that life forces on man by revealing to him gradually, as the years pass, the infinite degrees of imperfection in man's works, and at the same time, his inescapable duty to undertake them. These lectures are, then, only an attempt to bring together around a common thematic center—reality and poetry—a series of spiritual reactions that have been stimulated in my soul by many, many hours of enjoyment and illumination, of struggle and clarity, of questions and silences, that is, by many hours spent in reading and rereading some of Spain's greatest poets, in forgetting them and remembering them, many hours spent, in short, in living with their works.

1940   PEDRO SALINAS

TABLE OF CONTENTS

I

THE REPRODUCTION OF REALITY

Poem of the Cid

and

A Ballad

I

I propose to discuss, in these lectures, the attitude of the poet toward reality throughout Spanish poetry. I must add at once that I am using the word reality in a general and comprehensive sense: by it I mean all that lives outside of the poet, the material world which surrounds him, things, society, beings, all of life from a blade of grass to a moral doctrine elaborated over centuries. Reality, the life of the world that surrounds and limits us, that gives to the individual the measure, at once tragic and magnificent, of his own solitude and of his creative possibilities. Perhaps I should say too, to avoid confusion, that I am not referring to the so-called Spanish realism, although some of the inferences to be drawn from my opinions may apply to it. No, what I intend to consider here is a problem which I think should be the first to be examined in connection with every poet: the relation between his poetic world and the real world, the contact between external reality and his own inner, spiritual reality.

The poet is born into a world that is already made, amid a reality that is given to him and that forces itself upon him. If each poet were given the world in a plastic state, he would mold it in his own way and we could not even be sure that summer would come after spring. But fortunately the world is already made. And yet at the same time constantly to be made. The poet has as his object the creation of a new reality within the old reality. How will these two worlds come together, meet, how can they agree?

3

On the one hand a magnificent world, the material world, imperial with the majesty of sun and mountain, with the delicacy of the shell or the dragon-fly, imperial external reality. And on the other, a small spark, full of mystery and longing, flickering in a human mind that wants to use that outer reality only as a point of departure, as a springboard to the other reality within him. For me, poetry is nothing but the aggregate of relations between this psychological reality, strange and abnormal, the poetic soul, so exceptional and clairvoyant, and external reality, usual and ordinary, the reality of the outside world. And so, for me, the first thing that characterizes a poet is his way of perceiving reality, of according his own with that outer reality, in short, his attitude toward the world, which from his birth, surrounds him.

Reality is indispensable to the poet, but it alone is not enough. The real is a raw state. The world is a possibility, but it is incomplete and perfectible. Keats in a letter, in speaking of the beauty of a morning which tempts one to idle it away, writes: " The morning was right." And Guillén says: " The world is well made." What does this mean? Simply that reality must be revised, confirmed, approved by the poet. And he confirms or re-creates it by means of a word, by merely putting it into words. It is the poet's gift to name realities fully, to draw them out of that enormous mass of the anonymous. The poet who first sang the rose, in christening it, in naming it, gave it a new distinct life. Language itself is poetry. And the poet is therefore the one who uses languages best, who utilizes most completely its power of giving life to the anonymous, of giving a reality distinct and poetic to indistinct, crude reality. It is an error to say that the poet does not live in reality: he lives in it more than anyone else, more than the banker or doctor. It hurts him more, for he is peculiarly sensitive to it. The poet reacts to reality pretty much as the human organism reacts to air: man breathes in air, without which he cannot live, and so does the poet reality. Here then are two existing real things: lungs and air. How do they behave? The poet absorbs reality but in absorbing it reacts against it; and just as the air is breathed out after undergoing a chemical change in the lungs, reality is also returned to the world, transformed, in one way or another, by a poetic operation.

Poetry always operates on reality. The poet places himself before reality like a human body before light, in order to create something else, a shadow. The shadow is the result of the interposition of a body between light and some other substance. The poet adds shadows to the world, bright and luminous shadows, like new lights. All poetry operates on one reality for the sake of creating another. It cannot operate on a vacuum. So that the way a poet places himself, interposes himself between the radiant light of life and life itself will determine his peculiar way of being, his quality, that is, the form, the personality of his shadow. Nothing is complete without its shadow. Ever since the beginning of time poets have been creating realities of utmost purity, marvelous reflections, just as a tree in early spring covers a white wall with immaterial leaves of new springs taken from the real spring. Those who do not love shadows should never open a book of poetry. Things abound for those who prefer their concrete, raw substance. Let them eat, drink, embrace, touch. But when the enjoyment derived from embracing and touching material things is ended, another remains: the possession of a higher reality, raised to its ultimate impalpable category, shadows, the pure and luminous forms of the spirit.

Let us see now how some poets stand before the light called reality and then we shall know to what shadows they give eternal life. For that is the ultimate miracle of poetry: that matter dies, perishes, while the shadows remain and endure forever. That is why I intend to study Spanish poetry by observing the poetic attitude that our poets have taken toward reality.

The first and most elemental attitude of the poet toward reality is, it seems to me, to examine it, note it down, relate it. This is the epic form which observes life in motion, what has happened, and gives us the pure and simple product of that observation, although there is much in observation that may be personal. It is this plain, direct attitude that prevails in our earliest poetry.

Our poetry begins in the twelfth century. The first Spanish literary text is a poem: *Poema del Cid*. That first work seemed to give Spanish medieval literature its character. For three centuries the most important poetic production in Spain is narrative poetry in its various forms. While in France the lyric develops luxuriantly in two languages, while in Italy from the thirteenth century on, we have the *dolce stil nuovo*, and Petrarch and Dante create the great love lyric and poetry presenting a theological interpretation of the world, the Spanish poetic vein concentrates on the epic. Our oldest tradition is an epic tradition and this heritage has left an impress on all Spanish literature, as Menéndez Pidal has shown. Our first poets do not interpret, ask questions, idealize, but simply relate. They relate the historical realities closest to them. Their subject matter is drawn from historical feats, as is the case in a large part of medieval poetry. Everywhere as in Spain, medieval poetry is heroic poetry. But what is essentially distinctive of Spanish heroic poetry is its historical exactness. In its conception of this general creative form, the heroic, the narrative, we may perhaps find the first attitude of the Spanish poetic spirit to the reality called history. Reality in medieval Spain is feats, exploits: *cantar de gesta.* That is, exploits, actions. The other realities, the inner life, the world of feeling, non-heroic life, religious experience, scarcely exist as poetic matter, and when they do, it is in narrative form, too, as is the case in medieval Spanish religious poems. Reality is what happens, what occurs; it is action. It is not nature or feeling. And naturally, the way to convey that reality is to narrate it. But generally in doing this, heroic poetry begins to exercise its heroic function: it alters, exaggerates, idealizes reality to such an extent that mere deeds become heroic feats. Everything medieval, seen from a distance, seems heroic to us now; and all men, heroes. Life, though copied from reality, appears in a glorious aureole of light, the transfiguring light of poetic fancy. Medieval epic poetry,

to a large extent, fancies the historical. Let us see now
what Spanish poetry does with historical reality.

Our national hero, Rodrigo Dias de Vivar, the Cid, is
a man of flesh and bone, whose deeds we know with relative historical exactness. The poem, then, is founded on
the real existence of a man, is, as it were, a poetic bio-
graphy. This is the case in much of Spanish medieval
poetry, it starts from reality. And what does it do with it?
The *Poema del Cid* is not very extensive in comparison
with the great French *gestes*; it is only 3735 lines long. It
recounts to us the main part of the Castilian hero's life.
As you know, the Cid was sent into exile by the king of
Castile as a result of the calumny and slander of his enemies. The poem begins when the warrior leaves his home;
Vivar, with a handful of men, takes the road to Burgos.
He arrives at the city, and here the poet succeeds in conveying in a most effective and moving way all that exile
means. The Cid goes with his men to the house where he
usually stops in that city, but he finds the door shut fast.
The men call loudly and ask that it be opened but no
one answers. Then the Cid goes forward, takes his foot
from the stirrup and knocks at the door. And the poem
says:

> Yet the door would not open, for they had barred it fast
> *non se abre la puerta   ca bien era cerrada*

And at this moment the most unexpected thing happens.
A little girl, nine years old (marvelous and exquisite detail
of the poet, for the number adds to the scene an incredible
feeling of authenticity), a child appears from we know
not where and approaches the Cid:

But a maiden of nine summers came unto him at last
Una niña de nuef años   a ojo se parava

Let us imagine the scene for a moment: a group of warriors, with their long beards, fierce and weary, covered
with armor, on their horses. And there on the ground,
looking up at them a little girl, that is, the most tender
and innocent being conceivable, before that mass of men,
all force and iron. The child tells the Cid that the king
has ordered that no door be opened to the Cid under
penalty of forfeiting houses and lands and " to the very
eyes within the head " says the poet:

And, Cid, with our misfortune, naught whatever
    dost thy gain.
But may God with all his power support thee in
    thy pain:
Cid, en el nuestro mal   vos non ganades nada
mas el Criador vos vala   con todas sus vertudes santas

And the Cid with his men heeded that childish quivering
voice, which sounds in the poem like the form of his new
destiny, like the very voice of fate. Resigned, they spend
the night encamped outside the city. Until then they had
not perhaps realized fully what exile meant, nor all that
they would be denied. And they find it out from a child,
the child who is the first feminine character in Spanish
literature, the first woman mentioned and given form in
words in our literary language.

The Cid and his men decide to leave the kingdom within
the time allotted them. Now adventurous exploits will
begin. A living must be made. But how does the poem

express that seeking of a living, that task of traversing the world in search of a new horizon? Not with any high-sounding and heroic phrase or sentence, but in a very simple way, utterly humble and at the same time eternally human: to earn one's bread:

> de Castiella la gentil   exidos somos acá,
> si con moros non lidiáremos,   no nos darán el pan

The warrior does not leave in search of an ideal, or a mystery, or a fabulous enemy to be vanquished. The great human trial, the anxiety common to all, that elemental and primitive impulse which has spurred man from time immemorial, is the motivating impulse of the Cid too. Here you have reality, life seen face to face, without any idealistic or sentimental transformation. And there is another detail I should like to mention here too, another detail which shows us how the poem limits itself to the normal dimensions of life, to the warrior as seen, as observed directly, as a man. Throughout the poem, one word is repeated constantly, almost like a refrain: to ride. The Cid is continuously urging his men on: "Let us ride! We must ride!" And that word diffuses through the poem a certain dynamic impression, an impression of constant movement, and of the unending need to be alert, mounted on one's horse, in a continuous effort to conquer. What has since been called the struggle for life is expressed in our twelfth century poem by that expression, "we must ride." Man's destiny, his untiring exertion of effort, in short, the daily vital task performed with abnegation and humility, throbs in the *Poema del Cid*, in the simplest way possible, as a regular call to duty. By a strange association of ideas, often in reading a wonderful modern poem, in which all the subtlety and depth of contemporary thought have been concentrated, Paul Valéry's *Le Cimetière marin*, on coming to the famous invocatory line: " Debout, debout, il faut tenter de vivre! " I have recalled the words of that primitive poem, so simple and direct: "Onward, onward, we must ride." In our poem that invocation resounds like the call of a trumpet, calling the men to their vital task, exhorting them to go on living and to earn their living. And throughout Spain that verb *cabalgar* evokes the image of the complete medieval man, with his horse, the first man who distinguishes himself from the rest: the horseman.

In the remainder of the poem, the Cid continues to be a man of flesh and blood. The Cid, unlike other heroes of fiction or legend, has no mistress, no lady of his thoughts to whom to dedicate his sword. He is married and has two daughters. The Cid and his men ride to the monastery of San Pedro de Cardeña where he is to take leave of his family. They arrive at dawn and the abbot and monks come out to receive them. Finally Doña Jimena and her daughters appear. The lady falls to her knees before the Cid, weeping and wanting to kiss his hand. " Here we are," she says, " I and my daughters. We must separate. Give me your counsel." The Cid reaches down and lifts his daughters in his arms and presses them to his heart, for, says the poet, he loved them dearly. And the Cid replies to his wife:

Please God and sweet Saint Mary that yet upon a day
I shall give my girls in marriage with mine own hand
rich and well.

¡Plega a Dios   e a santa Maria,
que aun con mis manos   case estas mis fijas!

I need make no comment on these words, on this prayer
of the Cid for the future, but I cannot resist telling you
that in class once, while we were reading and commenting
on this passage, a very modern and emancipated student
said to me disdainfully: " So this is the hero? But he's
just a family man, a good bourgeois, with the ideals of a
stock-broker."

The Cid leaves his wife and daughter in the care of the
monastery. The moment of leavetaking arrives, an unforgettable moment in the poem. Do you know why? Because until now the poet has expressed himself in direct
manner, and now for the first time, in this state of emotional tension, as if all the normal and usual resources
had been exhausted and he felt the need to surpass the
ordinary forms of language with a new form that might
say more, express more, the poet creates the first metaphor,
the first image in Castilian poetry. And he writes:

As the nail from the flesh parteth, from each other did
they part.

assís parten unos d'otros   commo la uña de la carne.

This is the first flower in Spanish poetic language. The
first effort to say things in a different way, to seek in language the obscure paths that lead to poetic light. " As the
nail from the flesh." A brutal, harsh, violent metaphor.

A comparison between the suffering of the soul and acute physical pain. But expressed in words totally devoid of idealization, completely antiesthetic and with a human objectivity that would have delighted Flaubert.

The battles begin, the triumphs of the Cid, repeated again and again, told in great detail, which leave us with an impression of constant and painful exertion and not of miracles as in other medieval poems. Everything must be won inch by inch, through incessant combat. And in reading how preparations are made for one of these battles we come across the first nature description in our poetry. I shall quote it. Day is about to break. The poet expresses that fact in four clauses, in gradation, the first three descriptive, narrative:

> And now the dawn was breaking and the morning
> coming on,
> And the sun rising.
> *Ya crieban los albores   e vinie la mañana,*
> *ixie el sol, . . .*

We see in these three sentences the elemental use of language, to tell us something or present something to us, but it is used with delicate shadings: first dawn breaking, the presentiment or suspicion of light in the sky, then the coming of dawn, and finally the appearance of the sun. And what is the fourth sentence? Here there is no longer description or detail; feeling bursts forth in its simplest and most spontaneous form, in an exclamation:

> Very God! how beautifully it shone!
> *. . . ¡Dios, qué fermoso apuntava!*

Nothing more. Great though the development of this embryo has been, it must be said that in this seed of descriptive nature poetry is to be found all that came much later, in the renaissance and in romanticism. That is, the passage from nature perceived to nature felt, the transition from the descriptive to the lyric, from the observation in the first three sentences to the canticle in the last: " Very God! how beautifully it shone! " Which is, after all, a hymn to the sun, better than many later ones, much briefer and perfectly intelligible to everyone.

Little by little the Cid extends his conquests and crowns them with the capture of the beautiful city of Valencia which ends the period of trials and adversities. The struggle is over now. Then he sends for his wife and daughters and has them brought to Valencia. One of the most beautiful, yet simple, passages in the poem is the one describing the arrival of the ladies at Valencia. The Cid takes them up to the highest tower in the castle. They look down upon the very precious booty of their husband and father, the city of Valencia. And the poet says:

> And forth in all directions they turned their lovely eyes.
> *Ojos vellidos   catan a todas partes.*

Could one possibly express any better the admiration, joy, pride felt by the wife of the conqueror as her glance followed the horizon?

But the Cid's life has not yet earned him tranquillity. His anxiety now comes from what we might call a domestic worry, a family matter. The king, now reconciled with the Cid, wishes to honor him and proposes the marriage of his daughters with the Counts of Carrión, two nobles of the court that inspire no sympathy in the Cid. But since the king favors it, he accedes. His fears turn out to have been well founded. His sons-in-law are cowardly and perfidious; after a short stay in Valencia they leave with their wives for Castile, ostensibly, but, actually, for the sake of foul vengeance, and they abandon them after having beaten them up. A relative of the Cid who has been following them saves the young women. And the Cid goes to Castile to demand reparation of the insult, since it was the monarch who arranged the marriage. In a combat of honor the nobles of Carrión are defeated by the champions of the Cid. And in order that the reparation be even more complete, messengers arrive to ask the hand of his daughters for the princes of Aragon and Navarre, a much more honorable marriage than the first. And the poem says toward the end: "Today they are kinswomen unto the kings of Spain."

It is curious that the poem, after having developed the first part on a heroic plane, then takes a more limited, a more domestic, or as my student would say, a more bourgeois, subject. Why does he do this? The answer seems clear to me. The medieval warrior, from the moment that he is an object of poetry, changes at once from warrior to hero. His feats envelop him in a golden mist with the result that his human form is scarcely perceptible; it vanishes beneath the great, gigantic outlines and contours. The protagonist loses, we might say, his human stature and enters a higher category which is the product of poetic exaltation. The simply human is surpassed, banished by the new heroic dimension. Now the main characteristic of the *Poema del Cid* is its attachment, its fidelity to the consideration of the hero as man and nothing more than man. The tendency to exaggerate, to misproportion, is outweighed by the tendency to balance which is seen in the poet's desire to show us intimate aspects of the Cid's life, his human qualities and conflicts. He conquers Moors, takes Valencia, and by these very feats seems to leave us ordinary mortals and rise to the rank of superior beings. But then he suffers like a father and like a man, suffering for his daughters and the insult to his honor. And now he is on the same level with any father, and his situation and suffering can be understood and shared by anyone who feels paternal love, any ordinary man. The man who in the first part seemed to be lost in the fictitious, is returned to us in the last as a suffering and offended father, with the simplest human qualities.

I don't know if anyone will accuse me of lowering or detracting from the Cid or the *Poema* if I dare to suggest to you that while certain heroes like Roland leave the world on a tangent of idealized greatness and can only be conceived as beings of another world, the Cid remains in this one. And while I am insisting on the consideration of the Cid as a human being, virilely and strongly human, I should like to call your attention—since you live in a country like the United States—to how he made his way. He leaves Castile with a handful of men, without any other resources or means than his arms, his will and his faith. And little by little, through his own efforts, without the assistance, so common in medieval poems of chivalry, of miracles, of mysterious and supernatural forces, by the simple use of his manly strength, he makes over his life, captures Valencia, wins the esteem of Spain, wealth and honor. And I ask you—not, however, without fear of being accused of heresy by the Cid's idealistic admirers—isn't that what has been designated in America by an expression that never existed before, that arose here because the man it represented was born here, the man who is no product of chance, or favor, or miracle, but of his own works, the *self-made man?* Isn't this Castilian hero, the human hero par excellence, the first self-made man in our history and literature?

But there are still other facts that clarify further the attitude of our early poetry toward reality, the attitude of direct and simple observation, of faithful and true description. Menéndez Pidal, my greatly revered teacher, who as you know has been the incomparable discoverer and commentator of the Cid for the modern world, has shown, with the patience and precision of a great scholar, how faithful the poet is to history and geography, to the time and space of facts, that is, to reality. The poem has a considerable historical basis. Most of the characters are real; they were actually the Cid's friends and contemporaries, his companions, as in the *Poema.* Alvar Fáñez, Martin Muñoz, Muño Gustioz appear in documents of that time. The same is true of the enemies of the Cid, of the count Ansúrez as of his sons-in-law, the counts of Carrión. The principal facts that the poet tells us about the Cid's life are historically authentic. The Cid was an enemy of count García Ordóñez, he did suffer exile by order of the

King, he fought precisely at those places the poet men-
tions, he took Valencia and defended it against Yusuy;
one of his daughters married a prince of Navarre. There
is even a curious detail that confirms the biographical
authenticity. In several passages of the poem, the Cid,
according to a typically medieval custom, trusts in omens,
seeks the future in the superstitions held by the Middle
Ages. On leaving Vivar, he looks to see on what side the
crow is flying. You see, if it was on the right it was a
good sign, but, on the other hand, an evil omen if it flew
on the left.

> He saw birds of happy omen, as from the Jalón he passed.
> *al exir de Salón   mucho ovo buenas aves.*

This detail might be considered a conventional tag of the
period but it accords with documental proof, for in a Latin
document, in which an enemy challenges the Cid to a duel,
he is accused of trusting more in omens, in signs of birds
than in God.

And this fidelity to reality is just as evident in the geography. As Menéndez Pidal states, it has been possible to
identify all the place names in their modern or old forms.
At times a wood has disappeared, but it has been possible to
verify the fact that it had actually been at the place indicated. The poem describes all the roads taken by the Cid
and they correspond perfectly to what we know about the
ways of communication at that time, the Roman highways
and the secondary road from Burgos to Valencia. When
we are told about the capture of a small city, we are given
authentic information about its emplacement and the

strategy used so that we may better appreciate the military skill required of the Cid in taking it by surprise. And finally, even in the descriptive geography, we find amazing examples of veracity. The poet, in speaking of a town, Atienza, names it, then adds a phrase which locates and defines it materially: " Atienza, a great, strong rock." And as a matter of fact, now still we can see that town high up on a rock which looks as though it had been hewn by a pickax, and with a castle on its summit, giving the observer the precise impression of being a rock of great defensive strength; it could hardly be described with fewer or surer words than those used by the twelfth century poet.

If we continue this analysis of the poet's fidelity to reality by comparing the *Poema del Cid* with other medieval epics, we come upon the opinion expressed by the great admirer and translator of the poem into French, Damas Hinard. What he emphasizes most in his comparative study, is the absence in the Castilian poem of the unbridled imagination, incorrect proportions, scorn of the factual and the normal that abound in the French epic. Geography in the latter is imaginary. From time to time, fabulous beings, monsters, supernatural forces appear in the *Chanson.* When Roland blows his famous trumpet, it can be heard thirty leagues around. The superiority of the French in battle is such that five Frenchmen kill four thousand Moors. The poet is so eager to impress the reader that he violates the normal measures of reality which he changes to suit his needs.

What conclusions may we draw from all this? In the Middle Ages, historical reality, the account of the exploits of some person, may be handled in one of two ways. One is the chronicle, the dry, literal, historical work, the recording of facts without any kind of spiritual elaboration, that is, without any poetic creation, poetic vision. The other is the fictionization of reality, its transformation into an imaginary world in which reality is submerged and only appears from time to time between waves of fantasy in movement, of disordered imagination. The *Poema del Cid* is not a chronicle since its historical facts are raised to the category of poetic matter, and what interests us is not the fact, information or knowledge as historical, but the human life or lives that follow their course on a background of history. But it is not fictionization of reality either, like the French or German epics. It is reality to which a poetic character is given, reality made poetic; and we are constantly surprised by the balance and proportion maintained between facts presented by life, that is, material reality, and the act of creating from them a new poetic reality. We feel always in the poet a resistance to transfiguring changes, something I might call a consciousness of a certain level, a conscious will toward an end. And his end is to create a spiritual world, a spiritual reality by closely and affectionately observing the real world as the source of the poetic, as though he thought that from this constancy in following the source faithfully, step by step, poetry would spring.

What is then the first poetic attitude toward reality that we find in Spanish poetry? Direct perception and faithful reproduction. It is the reproductive attitude in the literal sense of the word. Life has produced certain things and beings. And the poet, captivated by their very existence, produces them over again poetically, re-producing them, that is, copying in his work of re-production the attributes, measures, form of the existing things created by Nature. He does not alter anything. It is the simplest poetic operation of all: reproducing, creating a spiritual world by submitting to the lines provided by the real model. It is conformity with reality, the simplest and most elementary form of maximum contact between reality and poetry. For the poet of the Cid, the poetic qualities of the hero are to be found in the real hero, in the sensible and visible manifestation of his deeds, just as for the sculptor of classical Greece, the goddess Venus, beauty, were in perfect conformity with the sensible forms offered by life in the body of woman. This explains the markedly classical character of the *Poema*. Not that Spanish literature is particularly classical in its character; it is much more likely to tend toward spiritual conventionalization or baroque convulsion. Perhaps the only example we can find in the history of Spanish art of an artistic conception similar to that of the *Poema del Cid* is the painting of Velázquez, those pictures painted five centuries later, upon which have fallen the injustice and limitation of a stupid adjective: realistic. When actually they are the most subtle, delicate and profound poetry of visible reality.

Reality had not yet been criticized, thought, it had not yet passed through the human mind as an object of meditation or judgment; it had not yet been submitted to the criterion of good or evil. It is pure and innocent. It simply *is*. This first primitive poetic attitude is to wonder at the world and to want to reproduce it. The poet of the Cid reacts like that child who attracted the attention of the poet Maragall so much: on looking at the Mediterranean one August afternoon, he exclaimed, " The sea! " And with this word he reproduced its beauty in his mind.

The *Poema del Cid* is the only example we have left of those long heroic, narrative poems called *cantares de gesta*. The other works of this type have disappeared. And the national poetic genius, the heroic spirit of the race is expressed in all its completeness two centuries later in the ballad, that form of poetry so characteristic of our literature. Everyone knows that a ballad is an epico-lyric poem, usually very short, of heroic or warlike character, and has an historical or legendary theme. It is poetry, naturally, written to be sung, anonymous, and subject to that process of elaboration, alteration, change, by the people that composed it, as it passes from mouth to mouth, from generation to generation. Every ballad had an author, of course, who first conceived and gave form to the poem. But once it is cast into the torrent of popular life, people consider it no longer as a perfect and finished work of art, but as a common good to be improved or embellished by all. And so most of our ballads have come down in numerous versions, each one of which is an attempt, a step toward the ultimate state which has found perfect and definitive expression. This treatment of the ballad, which Menéndez Pidal has called traditional, since it passes from father to son like a common poetic background, like a spiritual heritage, kept and preserved by all, is what gives our ballads their peculiar physiognomy. Another of its traits is its immense power of dissemination. So deep-rooted is this poetic form in the popular soul that we could define the boundaries of the great sixteenth century Spanish empire by simply studying the boundaries of the diffusion of the ballads. In other words: wherever a Spaniard went, a ballad went. The *conquistadores* took them to America and they were heard at the foot of the Andes. Today, today still, it is moving to hear the Jews of Spanish origin, descendants of those who were expelled by the Catholic King and Queen in 1492, sing ballads, in their archaic Spanish, in Salonika, Constantinople and Sophia. And both the victorious Spaniard, conqueror of the New World, and the vanquished Spaniard, the exiled Jew bound for the Orient, carried within their soul this poetry, the most completely popular of all, in its origin and in its deep-rootedness. Cultured people, clerics, the learned, scorned them, paid them not the slightest attention. An exquisite poet of the fifteenth century, the Marqués de Santillana tells us that only people of a low and servile condition enjoy ballads.

In Spain in the fifteenth century a learned and a popular muse exist side by side in the most curious way, completely separate from and ignorant of each other. But by the beginning of the sixteenth, ballads are printed and toward the middle of the century, the first collections are made and soon become popular. But by then the ballad was already dead as an essentially popular genre for the people no longer produced it; its day was done. However, it becomes known and circulates among cultured writers and

Spanish literature is enriched with a new family of ballads, artistic, literary ballads as opposed to old popular ballads. What I am about to say applies only, of course, to the old ballads.

According to Menéndez Pidal's theory, the first ballads are fragments of the *cantares de gesta*, the most important passages, those that left the deepest impression on the audience and were sung separately until they began to be considered separate works. Consequently, the content of the ballads, the subject-matter, is that of the medieval epic, French or Spanish, or the same as French poetic subject-matter of the period. They inherit the spirit and the artistic vision of the lost epic. The historical ballads would be, then, poetry derived from other poetry and celebrating over again some remote historical theme, as for example, the ballads about the Cid. But there is another group of ballads that does not merely remodel or make over old themes, but poetizes living history, contemporary reality. And it is this group that particularly concerns us here. The ballads referring to Don Pedro de Castilla were composed, according to Menéndez Pidal, during his lifetime. Even more interesting are the frontier ballads. You recall that the final struggle in the reconquest of the national territory is concentrated around Granada, the last Arabic kingdom in Spain. But the war is not a continuous or permanent war, a great war, but rather a series of attacks and military actions along the frontier between the Christian and Moorish kingdoms. The frontier ballads relate precisely the incidents in this struggle, individual exploits, acts of heroism, the taking of cities, but all in a series of isolated pictures, of partial views, always presented with heroic grace, and with romantic charm. Each episode in that war is by itself a subject of a poem; the ballad used it, immortalized it at the very moment it took place. It is a spontaneous poem, that springs up in the heat of battle and is inspired directly by reality. These ballads lack, naturally, the great sweep of the *cantares de gesta*, their magnificent mural painting, but they have, on the other hand, the vividness and concentration of things recently seen and lived, of fresh and vibrant impressions of real deeds. Besides, the brief and concise form of the ballad, which sometimes seems fragmentary, adds to its special poetic force and to its essential evocative intensity. It is a poem condensed into a small space and which expands as it enters our soul.

Let me illustrate with an example that will serve to corroborate what I said before about the first attitude of Spanish poetry to reality. It is the ballad of Alora, a city in the present province of Málaga, situated in a mountainous region. It is thirty-eight lines long and relates the death of the Governor Diego de Ribera during the siege of Alora through treason of the Moors. We are surprised first of all by its absolutely impersonal, we might almost say impassive, tone. The words transmit the facts to the reader with implacable informative rigor, without the poet's adding a single comment or an emotional accent. The poem is exactly what a glass is for the water in it: a form made of clear and transparent glass which holds the liquid without affecting its color or taste in any way. It has a limpidity, an integrity in its poetic apprehension of reality, insuperable in its purity and humility. But an analysis of the poem is no less instructive. We perceive at once the minute exactness of detail. In the first two lines we see the city designated by the words, "the well inclosed," and at once we imagine a walled city, "you who lie along the river." Alora is situated with very few words and with an extraordinary synthetic force: a city with walls on the bank of a river:

> *Alora la bien cercada,*
> *tú que estás en par del río*

The governor lays siege to it. But not on any day at all, the ballad does not omit this, on Sunday; not at any indefinite hour but in the morning precisely:

> *una mañana en domingo.*

The categories of time and space, the frames of reality, are defined thus at the very beginning of the poem and in the simplest way possible. Its authenticity, its factual truth, its reality are evident. With their artillery the Christians force an opening through the wall. The Moors, men and women, flee to the top of the castle, taking with them their transportable goods. But the poet specifies, determines what they take with them. The Moors do not flee so fast but that they have time to look over the things they are taking along and the poet enumerates them. The women, a typically feminine trait, take clothes as women would always do. The men take flour and wheat, the basis of material sustenance. The boys, raisins and figs, things to eat, too, but those especially liked by children because they are

sweet. And the young girls of fifteen carry off jewels and
gold:

> *Las moras llevaban ropa*
> *los moros harina y trigo,*
> *y las moras de quince años*
> *llevaban el oro fino,*
> *y los moricos pequeños*
> *llevan la pasa y el higo.*

In this distribution, in this exceedingly fine correspondence
or correlation between each person's load and his state of
being respectively man, woman, boy or girl, there is a
delicate skill more penetratingly realistic than any I have
ever seen in poetry. A Moor announces by waving a white
flag that the castle will surrender. Then the chief goes forward and trustfully raises the visor of his helmet. At that
moment a Moor shoots an arrow at him and pierces his
head. And two of his followers pick him up. Not two
anonymous men, no. The poet tells us their names: one
is Pablo, the other, Jacobillo, two gentlemen that he had
reared in his home since their childhood:

> *Sacolo Pablo de rienda,*
> *y de mano Jacobillo,*
> *esos dos que había criado*
> *en su casa desde chicos*

Ever the same desire for precision, exactness and fidelity in
transcribing the facts. The last four lines tell briefly of his
death. The wounded man is carried to the doctors' just in
case he may be cured but after a few words he declares
his testament, that is, his last will. And so the poem ends.

It does not say he died. It avoids the direct expression and uses in its place a completely impersonal and realistic periphrase: he declared his testament to them. Death is stripped of its dramatic character. And the poem ends. It ends as it began, with that absolutely crystalline purity and with that vividness that leaves one the impression of having been an eye-witness of the events related.

I have often asked myself in the face of the deep and simple emotion this poem arouses: where is the poetry? Not a metaphor, not a single fact emphasized. A simple exposition of some event, in precise proportion and in the smallest number of words possible. The event in itself has no special interest, a betrayal at war like so many others. Only that felicitous distribution of goods among the poor people as they flee gives a slight suggestion of personal intervention in the poem. And, of course, the answer is easy. The poetry is not to be found in the theme, which is common enough, not in the choice of words, nor in the idealization of any gesture or action. It is simply in the attitude of the poet to his subject. In the objective neatness of the perception, in the extremely faithful transmission to the poem of all that the eye contemplated. It is an attitude of respect, of absolute conformity with the facts and traits furnished by life. It is, even more than the *Poema del Cid,* more completely faithful in its observation of reality and more intense in its religious reverence for reality. Poetry and reality are in complete accord, without any previous doubt or conflict, without any hesitation or analysis. Life is reproduced as it is seen. It is a religious, perhaps simple but nevertheless

deep, sense of reality. In short, for this poetic vein of
Spanish medieval poetry, reality is an absolute value, it
is the highest value. To poetize is to re-produce. The
poetic operation is primitive and elemental: to give names
to things and acts, to translate them into words, let them
be impelled by their own real force through language,
without any alteration. In this poetry, man's spirit appears to us a state of paradisaical innocence and purity,
before sin. The sin is thought, the application to that objective marvel, the world, that product of man, analysis,
doubt, interrogation. There is no questioning. There is
pure existence, presence of reality, "adamic" poetry,
poetry of the first vision of the world that surrounds us.
It is an attitude toward the reality that *is*, the pure, primitive attitude par excellence. This attitude may seem more
or less simple to us today, more or less bare, if we com-
pare it with the wealth created by other poetic attitudes
since. But we shall always look back at it, at least I do, with
nostalgia as for a paradise lost, for a virgin world where
reality and poetry lived in peace and effortless conformity
within the soul of man, or rather perhaps, where war had
not yet been declared between reality and poetry, a war
which came later and which will never cease in the spirit
of poets, in their attitude toward the world. Let us leave
then, exiles that we are, this earthly and poetic paradise,
this paradise of unity.

II

THE ACCEPTANCE OF REALITY

Jorge Manrique

Calderón de la Barca

II

In Spain, during the fifteenth century, poetry follows two distinct and parallel courses. One is that of the popular ballad which is poetry of war and history—we might call it poetry of the past—full of heroes and echoes of battles and great feats. But in the courts and palaces a new spirit had been diffused, which precisely because it found favor with the people of the court, was called courtly. This courtly spirit aspired to a highly refined and cultured conception of life. Those who share it are, to be sure, warriors, ballad heroes from time to time. But because of that need of man to be what he is not, to escape from his ordinary state, the same men who fought hard, heavily armed, who were capable of the most cruel acts, once they were back at court, took delight in a gallant and exquisite kind of life, in which gentleness and delicacy replaced the rudeness of war. The same hand that had worn an iron glove now wore the most dainty, perfumed glove. This courtly poetry of the fifteenth century has always seemed to me something like a glove, nicely made, of fine leather, and used to conceal the natural claw-like form of the hand. Though man has lived for many centuries, his hand has never lost its anatomical character of talon. The glove hides and disguises it, stylizes it, lends it a momentary gentleness. So this fifteenth century courtly poetry seems to me a glove that knights wore so that when they extended a hand to the ladies, the natural hardness of bones and muscles would not be too apparent. For, actually, this poetry was like a hand extended to ladies. Compared with the wide range and the broadly human appeal of the poetry of action which was directed to all, this courtly poetry which came to Spain naturally, as the last historical consequence of the Provençal poetry of the Troubadours, is indeed a poetry of limited scope. For me, its very name spells its essential limitation: courtly, that is, of a special social circle, of a single class, and directed toward the sentiments of that class.

And what were those class sentiments? One, mainly, love. Love in the courtly manner, too, that is, as a subtle literary theme that could be elaborated with the delicacy and exquisiteness of embroidery. The amorous sentiment in the Middle Ages, under the pressure of Petrarchan mysticism and Provençal subtlety, attains such extremes of intellectual refinement, of conventionalized elegance, that it is left bloodless, pale and weak. Fire, passion, sincerity flee, terrified. And all we have left is a casuistic and rhetorical conception of love, a divagation through gardens of love, gardens so exquisitely drawn that the tracery, the complicated and ingenious intersection of lines, becomes far more prominent than the slight natural element that one assumes exists under it. Poetry of arabesques. Love is used by these poets as line is by the Arabic designer: as the means of yielding to the capricious fantasies of decorative ingenuity in order to cover a surface with intricate interlacing curves. A poet of the fifteenth century, Juan de Mena, called his work *Labyrinth*. All this courtly poetry is a labyrinth, in which ladies and gentlemen play hide-and-seek, a labyrinth without exit, outlined with trim and fragrant myrtles, and out of which no one ever comes into the full light of day. This kind of poetry is found in Spain in collections called *Cancioneros,* many of them enormous anthologies that include many poets. And yet, at the very core of this artificial poetry, we come upon the most profound, grave, sincere poet produced by the Spanish Middle Ages.

His name was Jorge Manrique. He came of a family of powerful Castilian nobles and was born about 1440. The Castilian nobles of that time were divided into irate factions that reflected the cupidity of the Court. Spain was passing through one of its worst periods. The national forces were exhausting their energy in factional strife, in fratricidal war, instead of ending the war of Reconquest. The nobles aspired to power, wealth, maximum influence at court, and to becoming as strong or stronger than the King. And royal favor determined fortune and misfortune, ruin or elevation in rank. So that Jorge Manrique, from his very birth, was involved in a net of palace intrigues and conflicts with other nobles. And of the four campaigns in which we know him to have participated, in no one of them did he fight against his natural and secular enemy, the Moors, but against other parties of nobles, always in the service of the king against whom they had risen. In 1479, the Marqués de Villena, rebelling against royal authority, engaged in a violent war with the Catholic Monarchs. Jorge Manrique, in the service of the latter, attacked a castle that was being defended by the troops of the marquis, and carried away by his imprudent valor, met with death at the age of thirty-nine.

What did he leave behind him? A small number of poems, one single poem. Only fifty of his love poems have been preserved. And all of them are short, perfect expressions of the platitudes of the time, without any personal or original accent. Poems of a school, made according to the pattern of the period; no one could perceive behind these rimed subtleties a man or a poet. Yet Jorge Manrique was a man and a great poet. He was a great poet only once, but in such a way that he will endure forever. In 1476 his father died, Don Rodrigo Manrique. And Jorge wrote the Stanzas commemorating the death of his father, known since under the title of *Coplas por la muerte de su padre*. This poem represents without a doubt the greatest height attained by the elegiac lyric in our language. So vastly superior is it to all the rest that Jorge Manrique is one of the strangest and most disconcerting cases found in the history of poetry. Poetic phenomena have always been complicated and obscure. It is difficult to explain why some works are poetry and others are not, why one man writing on a given theme, impelled by certain spiritual stimuli, creates a work of art, while another draws nothing new out of the mysterious. One continues to ask: why are some men poets and not others? But what is more baffling is how these two qualities, that of being and not being a poet, the creating of a work and the writing in a vacuum, can coexist in the same being in a state of absolute separation.

For in the case of Manrique, it is not a question of youthful works which foretell what will come later; there is no gradual spiritual preparation of the work within a soul, as of light within the heart of the night. It is impossible to conceive of unity in the poetic soul of Manrique. In his case, perhaps better than in that of anyone else, the question presents itself: is the poet the product of accident or destiny? Is he merely a vital effort, uncertain and wavering, a throw of the dice upon the absolute, which will win only if mysterious and unforeseeable circumstances—which we so stupidly call chance—concur? Or is he a form of the world's will, which acts from the moment that his sensibility and reason perform on what is placed before him, to a greater or lesser degree? Is the poetic soul a general aptitude for being moved by a rose or a mountain, suffering or sensuality, yet independent of these poetic themes of the world, or is it a very special and limited capacity like an instrument that will play only if a particular hand touches it? Of course, every poet usually has a sphere of poetic action, a climate particularly suited to the full expansion of his being. But when he is transported to other climates, he takes with him, if not all his greatness, at least glorious traces and echoes of it, reflections of his great and peculiar light. In Manrique, the division is clear-cut. From absolute darkness to the radiant appearance in the *Coplas por la muerte de su padre* of one of the most beautiful and resplendent lights in universal poetry. But let me explain the mystery. A great Spanish poet of the nineteenth century, Bécquer, compared genius with a harp, asleep in a dark corner of a salon, its chords full of marvelous notes awaiting " a hand of snow that may awake them." Jorge Manrique's case is a perfect illustration of Bécquer's harp. He spent most of his life asleep,

in a courtly salon. And two years before his death he
found the mysterious hand, the real hand of snow since it
was the hand of death, that awakened all the slumbering
music so that we shall never forget it.

Jorge Manrique's father was the great noble of his day.
He fought much during his life, triumphed over enemies
and adversaries, attained great honors, the greatest of all
of which was that of Grand-Master of the most important
military order, the order of Santiago. Jorge, the poet, was
his fourth son. The grand-master died at the age of
seventy, after a human life crowded with effort, struggle
and victory. And the son wished to commemorate the
figure of his father in these lines. We see thus that the
point of departure of the poem is a direct vital event and
one common to all human beings: the loss of the person
who gave us life. Jorge Manrique's elegy starts, unlike the
love poems, not from an exaggeration of reality, not
like other poems of this type from a general consideration of the loss called death, that is, from an abstraction
of reality, but from a simple human fact. It is, from the
beginning, a poem taken from reality. Let us see how the
poet treats it. Perhaps we should say here that the elegy is
a short poem made up of forty 12-line stanzas, that is, less
than 500 lines long.

The first thing that elicits our admiration is the perfect
balance between the real fact that occasioned the poem,
the death of Don Rodrigo, his father, between the cause
or circumstance and the profound human generality and
universal significance to which the poet rises from this
circumstance. Actually, it is only a matter of commemo-

rating the death of a man, and the poet does this, telling us in detail what he was like and what he did. But grief works on the soul of Jorge Manrique with so purifying and elevating an effect, that from the pure feeling of grief arises a sort of philosophical serenity, of superior contemplation of all suffering in life and in men.

We should observe at once that the point of view with regard to life is essentially different from that of the narrative poetry, limpid, innocent, direct, without questioning or doubt. The poem of Jorge Manrique is quite the contrary: life, the reality of the world have already become the object of a deeper, more penetrating, scrutinizing glance, of disquieting interrogations by a spirit anxious over its destiny. The analytical mind has performed on the beautiful body of the world that work of dissection or autopsy to which man is fatally drawn during certain periods of his mental and historical life. In the ballads and in the *Poema del Cid*, we seemed to hear: " Here is life. Take it." In Jorge Manrique we hear: " What is life? " That's why we stop on coming to this poem in the history of the Spanish lyric as before the first imperative voice of a mystery saying " Halt! " Man has already begun to look at reality with eyes that are not satisfied with surfaces or with the appearances of things; he has left behind, with conviction, the beautiful forms of life, its pleasures and delights; he has chosen the dark road inward, the road of the inner life, the road which leads man to see the other side of things, the terrible reverse of the world. Jorge Manrique takes the first step in our lyric toward the inner life and its anguish, he goes straight without hesitation to

4

the core, the intimate conflict of every spiritual life. Let us see how he takes the journey, what he gathers from it and the doctrine he conveys to us.

The first stanza is an exhortation to the soul to awaken from its slumber to see how silently life passes, how imperceptibly, and how death approaches. Pleasure, flower of a moment, is in recollection only pain:

> O let the soul her slumbers break,
> Let thought be quickened, and awake;
> Awake to see
> How soon this life is past and gone
> And death comes softly stealing on,
> How silently!
>
> Swiftly our pleasures glide away,
> Our hearts recall the distant day
> With many sighs;
> The moments that are speeding fast
> We heed not, but the past,—the past,
> More highly prized.

> *Recuerde el alma adormida,*
> *Avive el seso, y despierte*
> *Contemplando*
> *Cómo se pasa la vida,*
> *Cómo se viene la muerte*
> *Tan callando.*
> *Cuán presto se va el placer,*
> *Cómo después de acordado*
> *Da dolor,*
> *Cómo a nuestro parecer*
> *Cualquiera tiempo pasado*
> *Fué mejor.*

And if that is so, we must decide that what will come will
be like what has past. Here Manrique formulates one of
the most desolating thoughts conceivable:

> Onward its course the present keeps,
> Onward the constant current sweeps,
> Till life is done;
> And, did we judge of time aright,
> The past and future in their flight
> Would be as one.

> *Y pues vemos lo presente*
> *Como en un punto es ido*
> *Y acabado,*
> *Si juzgamos sabiamente*
> *Daremos lo no venido*
> *Por pasado.*

The present flees from us, escapes. Recalled, it is painful.
But the future, one might ask, and man always does ask?
And Manrique answers, " If we are wise, on seeing how
the present vanishes and ends, we shall consider the future as past. No one should deceive himself into thinking that what will come will last longer than what has
past." And so he shuts man's only door of escape, the hope
in what has not yet taken place, the dawn of the future, in
short, the door to the possible, to the incalculably possible. On finishing these stanzas one feels like a prisoner,
shut up without possible exit, within the three dimensions of time, past, present and future, which may be
reduced to one single truth: fugacity, transiency, nothing.
Our lives are compared to rivers carried to the sea into
which flow brooks and great streams alike; death is the
great final sea, equalizer of human destinies. And all this

is said by the poet in the gravest, simplest way, without the slightest indication of complaint or wavering, as if he were above the weakness of feeling.

However, the poet, in order to convince us of the veracity of his statement, does not wish to confine himself to this doctrinal assertion, too abstract and lofty perhaps. So now he descends to life with us, to reality, and reviews one by one all the things of this world, what man values most, what gives him greatest delight and he will reveal to us what there is behind it all. The poet begins, effectively enough, with physical beauty as seen in a lovely and fresh complexion. As a sign of what is most valued in the world, a feminine face appears in the stanzas of Manrique, a face as clear and fresh as early morning. But that freshness of the body, that rosy color are nothing: for in old age they vanish. Everything becomes weight, heaviness. Nobility, pride in family are no more secure, they go too. And as for high rank, wealth, to whom do they belong? To him who owns them? Not at all. The poet says: "To a lady of fickle heart, inconstant." None other than Dame Fortune who changes everything with her ever-revolving wheel. There remain, perhaps, the pleasures and delights of this life. But they are only lying messengers, fleet coursers, sent by death in ambush to deceive us:

> The pleasures and delights, which mask
> In treacherous smiles life's serious task,
> What are they all,
> But the fleet coursers of the chase,
> And death an ambush in the race,
> Wherein we fall?

No foe, no dangerous pass, we heed,
Brook no delay, but onward speed
With loosened rein;
And when the fatal snare is near,
We strive to check our mad career,
But strive in vain.

Los placeres y dulzores
De esta vida trabajada,
Que tenemos,
¿Qué son sino corredores,
Y la muerte es la celada
En que caemos?
No mirando a nuestro daño
Corremos a rienda suelta
Sin parar;
Des que vemos el engaño
Y queremos dar la vuelta
No hay lugar.

Here the poet feels a sort of sensual thrill, almost a temptation: he says that on seeing them we rush madly toward them with loosened rein. How perfectly this expression conveys the eagerness, the impetuosity with which human appetite dashes forward in search of its satisfaction! How one perceives in this one phrase something like a new horizon, a start, a violent gust that drives us on! But soon we see our error. And then we cannot turn back, there is no way back. Pleasure has allured us to its abyss, to its deceitful illusion. But perhaps the reader might not believe these things hearing them thus as mere assertions of disillusioned doctrine. He must be convinced with examples taken from the world, from reality itself. He must see before his eyes the spectacle of all that has been thought great and happy in the world.

That is a method commonly used in moral philosophy, the dramatization of the example. But Manrique uses it in an exceedingly ingenious and effective way, in which I see a sure realistic instinct. In cases like this, the moralist usually has recourse to examples from antiquity, to persons of universal historical renown. But Manrique looks for a way more likely to impress the men for whom he is writing, his contemporaries of the fifteenth century. So he says: let us leave the Greeks and Romans alone and look to our own time, our own house. Let us not fix our glance on remote ages that we never saw, on beings that we never knew, and whose disappearance, after all, might seem perfectly natural to us. Then begin those marvelously evocative stanzas, perhaps the finest in the poem, overflowing with beautiful and moving reality. He evokes the court of John II of Castile who died when the poet was a young man. This evocation adopts a form often used in medieval poetry: the question asking what has become of something past, where it ended. It is the form made famous by Villon in " Mais où sont les neiges d'antan? " This part only occupies 24 lines, but so dense are they with evocative realism, that we have a complete picture of all of a luxurious and delightful life. The poet does not describe, he merely enumerates, much as a captain calls the roll of his soldiers. The poet calls the roll of the phantoms recently past. And we see before us ladies, gowns, perfumes, head-dresses. Then come the jousts and tournaments, palace entertainment, the attire of knights, plumes in their helmets, even to the ornaments on their clothes. The sound of music sung caresses the ear, and in the last stanza, we even hear the echo of dancing at balls.

> Where is the King, Don Juan? Where
> Each royal prince and noble heir
> Of Aragon?
> Where are the courtly gallantries?
> The deeds of love and high emprise,
> In battle done?
>
> Tourney and joust that charmed the eye,
> And scarf, and gorgeous panoply,
> And nodding plume,
> What were they but a pageant scene?
> What but the garlands, gay and green,
> That deck the tomb?
>
> Where are the high-born dames, and where
> Their gay attire, and jewelled hair,
> And odors sweet?
> Where are the gentle knights, that came
> To kneel, and breathe love's ardent flame,
> Low at their feet?
>
> Where is the song of Troubadour?
> Where are the lute and gay tambour
> They loved of yore?
> Where is the mazy dance of old,
> The flowing robes, inwrought with gold,
> The dancers wore?
>
> *¿Qué se hizo el Rey Don Juan?*
> *Los infantes de Aragón,*
> *¿Qué se hicieron?*

¿Qué fué de tanto galán,
Qué fué de tanta invención
Como trujeron?
Las justas é los torneos,
Paramentos, bordaduras
E cimeras,
¿Fueron sino devaneos?
¿Qué fueron sino verduras
De las eras?
¿Qué se hicieron las damas,
Sus tocados, sus vestidos,
Sus olores?
¿Qué se hicieron las llamas
De los fuegos encendidos
De amadores?
¿Qué se hizo aquel trovar,
Las músicas acordadas
Que tañían?
¿Qué se hizo aquel danzar
Y aquellas ropas chapadas
Que traían?

What a deep impression is left on our fantasy by this sober and austere poem of a smiling world, of a frivolous world in which pleasure appears in graceful forms, in elegant gestures, in music, in love! Precisely because the evocation is so rapid, we feel all that is pathetic in its passing, and the rapid strokes of the poet suggest the rapidity with which everything passes in the world. For after asking ourselves what became of all that—not of a remote paradise about which we'd only heard, but of a vital procession that many could have seen—the poet responds:

Where shall we seek them now? Alas
Like the bright dewdrops in the grass,
They passed away.

¿Dónde iremos a buscallos?
¿Qué fueron sino rocíos
De los prados?

A wonderful comparison, between a delicate and pleasurable existence, an extravagant life of love and sensuality, with these drops that quiver a moment in the morning, crystalline, reflecting the lights in the world in their short life, and that then are destroyed in the heat of the sun.

Then he goes on to show how death undoes the grandeur of kings, of great nobles, of so many dukes, counts and marquises with a single breath. And not even those things which represented maximum strength to the Middle ages, armies with their waving banners, castles, thick walls, nay, the most solid fortifications are of no avail against inexorable death. And so he says to death, after enumerating all these kinds of power:

All these cannot one victim keep
O Death from thee
When thou dost battle in thy wrath
And thy strong shafts pursue their path
Unerringly.

¿Qué aprovecha?
Cuando tú vienes airada
Todo lo pasas de claro,
Con tu flecha.

In reading this stanza, I have always thought of Jorge Manrique's death in action. He, the author of this metaphor on the sweeping power of death, saw an arrow come and penetrate his perishable body, and thus confirmed in his flesh the vision written two years before, of a sharp, mysterious power that comes down from heaven against the human breast.

In the following stanzas the element of concrete, historical reality recurs: he gives us a brief account of his father's life, his exploits, his adversities and his fortitude in the face of them, comparing him with the greatest men. And then comes the final scene, of an inimitable grandiose simplicity. On ending the recital of his father's life, the son tells us that after his father had exposed his life for his king a great many times, death came to knock at his door in a battle. He even gives us the exact geographical place: death appeared in his own town of Ocaña. Here is another example of what I mentioned in the beginning, of concrete reality which Jorge Manrique uses so skilfully as he alternates it with abstract and general ideas. That mere naming of Ocaña, a city in the province of Toledo, gives the poem a kind of weight, authenticity, earthly solidity that contrasts with the loftiness and elevation of the philosophical reflections. It is the eternal Spanish faculty of not losing contact with the earth, that inescapable need which our national soul seems to feel to put a ballast into fancy, to remind us that matter, the force of gravity are present in man always, even when he is dreaming the most wonderful dreams. And now the poem uses the dramatic and allegorical form for a moment. Death enters and speaks: she invites the gentleman to look at her without fear, to behave in this last battle as valiantly as in all the rest, for after it will come the triumph most precious to Christians: eternal life. Don Rodrigo does not hesitate, waver or complain. On the contrary, he is ready to die with joyful, clear, pure willingness, simply because it would be madness for man to want to live when God has determined otherwise. In this symbolical dramatization, the poet has taken us back to abstract art, to the world of representative images. But continuing the play of alternatives, reality again appears in the last stanza. My father died, he says, with all his senses, encircled by his wife, children, brothers and servants. A moment ago the nobleman was engaging in a dialogue with death in a symbolical world; now we see him as in an engraving, an engraving representing the death of a medieval knight, with his family around his bed to receive his last breath. The exact, direct, humble vision of life crowns this poem so replete with generalizations, symbols and ideas.

Let us resume now. What is the attitude of the poet to reality? First, one of severe and implacable scrutiny: life, pleasures, vanities are all as nothing. This world is but a road to another. Philosophical penetration seems, for a moment, to take from life its last ray of hope and faith. But the serenity of the Christian soul does not allow rebellion or despair. The world is like that, to be sure. But the poet says in stanzas 5 and 6: that does not prevent our facing it with dignity. One needs good judgment, says Jorge Manrique, to make this brief and deceitful journey without erring; it would be well to use it.

This world is but a highway going
Unto that other, the abode
Without a sorrow;
The wise are they who gird them, knowing
The guideposts set along the road
Unto tomorrow.

Este mundo es el camino
Para el otro, que es morada
Sin pesar;
Más cumple tener buen tino
Para andar esta jornada
Sin errar.

Did we but use it as we ought
This world would school each wandering thought
To its high state.

Este mundo bueno fué
Si bien usásemos de él
Como debemos.

That is the last conclusion: we must not let ourselves be deceived by apparent and misleading reality, but rather make good use of it. We must not disdain it because all is false in it, but live it valiantly, utilize well those appearances, for at the end of them is eternal life, salvation. It is the purest poem on the dignity of life. It is the conception of life of a Christian gentleman. Centuries later, Calderón, in *La Vida es Sueño*, treats the same problem in dramatic form. Is life a dream, a deceptive appearance, nothing more? Can man have any certainty that he lives? No, perhaps not. But nevertheless, just in case life should be real, we should live it well and honorably, not flee from it or loathe it. It is an attitude of being in perfect conformity with reality, of its full and valiant acceptance. This elegy most beautifully exemplifies it. For when the poet represents death calling the nobleman and his pure, voluntary acceptance of death, we see the greatest, the most heroic acceptance of reality and life. Only he who accepts his end, death, can be said to be in accord with life, can be said to have accepted life in its most terrifying dimension, that of being a transitory gift and a very perishable one.

In his magnificent book, " The Waning of the Middle Ages," Huizinga says:

The dominant thought, as expressed in the literature, both ecclesiastical and lay, of that period, hardly knew anything with regard to death but these two extremes: lamentation about the briefness of all earthly glory, and jubilation over the salvation of the soul. All that lay between—pity, resignation, longing, consolation—remained unexpressed and was, so to say, absorbed by the too much accentuated and too vivid representation of Death hideous and threatening. Living emotion stiffens amid the abused imagery of skeletons and worms.

Now then, the elegy of Jorge Manrique is the exception to that general tone found in the sentiment of death in the fifteenth century. No egoism, no attachment to earthly things. Death is not considered the worst of all evils, but a good which is joyously accepted. Death is consoling, more even, liberating. And what Huizinga does not find, misses, is to be found, in utter completeness, in this superb poem on death as a passage to a higher life.

We shall not find this attitude expressed in Spanish literature again with the same simplicity and austerity. But in the seventeenth century, a work, whose conception is of insuperable grandeur, treats the same theme and the same vital solution, magnificently expressed, in dramatic form. It is *La Vida es sueño* by Calderón de la Barca. Two centuries had passed since Manrique. The Renaissance had passed over human consciousness discovering continents, altering beliefs, widening enormously human horizons. Man feels better, knows more, expresses with greater exactness and beauty his inner life. But he pays for all that. He pays with what man has been paying, century by century, for his growing spiritual conquests, namely, with an ever greater complexity of mind, with an ever more dramatic sense of the conflict between world and man, with the enormous weight of the contemplation of life, hitherto so pure and simple, as a problem. The man of 1640, Calderón, is a much more complicated human organism than the man of 1470, Manrique. The conflict is the same; the anguish of the soul in facing it is identical; and the solution is the same. The lyric poet and the dramatist coincide in their point of departure and in their conclusion. But what the lyric poet of the fifteenth century resolves in 400 lines, with a single line of thought clearly and simply expressed, takes the dramatist of the seventeenth century three acts of complicated action in dazzling language. And what the poet saw purely and directly, the dramatist sees across a whole new scaffolding of intricate concepts. It is the baroque.

The action takes place in Poland. The king there, Basilio, is much given to astrology and consulting the stars. When his son Segismundo is born, the most terrifying omens occur: there is an eclipse, the heavens are dark, buildings shake and stones rain from the clouds. His mother dies in giving birth to him. Basilio has recourse to his studies and from them deduces that his son will be the most violent man, the most cruel prince that has ever lived, and that one day he will see himself at his feet humiliated by him. Then he decides not to report his birth, to keep him hidden, to shut him up in a cave as a prisoner where he will be unable to give free rein to his evil instincts as foretold by the stars. He does this. In the first act, we see Segismundo in a tower, chained, and dressed in skins. His monologue is the most famous in our literature. It is the desperate cry against life as he knows it, in chains. It is the lamentation of the innocent man who does not know why he is in such a state. And seeing himself chained while the wild animals around him remain free, he asks the famous question that has been and will be echoed in so many human consciences:

> And with so much more of a soul
> Must I have less liberty?
> ¿Y teniendo yo más alma
> Tengo menos libertad?

The first conclusion at which Segismundo arrives in this awful soliloquy is that the only cause of man's suffering, his only blame is life itself:

> Though for being born I feel
> Heaven with me must harshly deal,

Since man's greatest crime on earth
Is the fatal fact of birth.

Bastante causa ha tenido
vuestra justicia y rigor,
pues el delito mayor
del hombre es haber nacido.

Segismundo's first contact with reality could not be more
disheartening: reality is a sentence, a prison, like the one
he lives in, seeing how the other beings, animals, enjoy
their existence in liberty.

But at the very beginning of the play, Basilio, who from
time to time feels remorse for what he has done to his son,
decides to give him the chance of showing, by his acts,
whether the stars were right in foretelling his savage
nature, and thus to end his doubts as to whether he has
done well or ill in shutting him up. To this end he has
a narcotic given to Segismundo, and while he is still
drugged, has him brought to the palace and placed in a
sumptuous chamber surrounded by people who will treat
him like a prince in order to see how he behaves. In short,
Segismundo is put to a test without knowing it and on
this test will depend his future and his father's decision.
The result could hardly be more disastrous. The man-
beast awakens and finding himself in that sumptuous reality, vents his passions without disguise or restraint. His
fresh will, free for the first time, expresses itself in the
wildest desires: he heeds no advice, insults the nobles,
tries to force an embrace on a lady, ends by throwing a
servant out of the window simply because he opposes
his wishes. His father enters, doubtless confident that

Segismundo will bow to his authority. But his son answers his reproaches with the greatest ferocity, saying that
his father is to blame for the way he is since he had him
brought up like a savage, that he is not grateful to him
for giving him life, since though he gave it to him, he
took it back by denying him its highest attribute, liberty.
And the father who came to blame his son, finds himself
blamed, the advantageous role of accuser having passed
to the accused. A fine scene this is, in its period. Apart
from its particular interest in the story, seen by itself, one
feels behind the words of father and son a wider and
deeper conflict: through the mouth of Segismundo, the
maltreated man of all time speaks, all the men who have
been given life but not liberty, all the socially chained. In
Segismundo, what you call the under-dog speaks. And it
is very curious to realize that right in the midst of the
Catholic monarchy of Spain, the most absolute and aristo-
cratic of all, a monarchical and Catholic poet makes a character utter the most violent and persuasive defense of
man's right not only to life, but to liberty. In the words
of Segismundo, that seem to be only the defense of a son
abused by a powerful father, all the natural rights of man
are being defended. But Basilio promptly decides that the
stars were right, that his son is a wild beast, that he must
be returned to solitude. He threatens him saying:

> Yet be warned, and on thee take
> Ways more mild and beseeming,
> For perhaps thou art but dreaming,
> When it seems that thou'rt awake.

5

Mira bien lo que te advierto:
que seas humilde y blando,
porque quizá estás soñando,
aunque ves que estás despierto.

From this moment on, doubt is sown in Segismundo's soul. Dream? But doesn't he touch, see? No, he is dreaming. He has become aware of what he is, part man, part beast. And in these words we have Segismundo's second vision of reality: the evil that man is born with, the enslaving power of the instincts.

The father's plan is carried out. Segismundo is drugged again and taken back to his prison. There he awakens chained and dressed in skins as before. His counsellor tells him that all the things he thought he saw were merely a dream and that he had not left the tower. A strange light appears in Segismundo's mind. If what he saw and touched had been a dream, why should this that he now touches and sees be reality? Isn't this probably like the other merely a dream, merely an illusion?

> Nor even now am I awake
> Since such thoughts my memory fill,
> That it seems I am dreaming still:
> Nor is this a great mistake;
> Since if dreams could phantoms make
> Things of actual substance seen,
> I things seen may phantoms deem.
> Thus a double harvest reaping,
> I can see when I am sleeping,
> And when walking I can dream.

> *Ni aun agora he dispertado;*
> *que según Clotaldo entiendo,*

todavía estoy durmiendo;
y no estoy muy engañado,
porque, si ha sido soñado
lo que ví palpable y cierto,
lo que veo será incierto;
y no es mucho que rendido,
pues veo estando dormido,
que sueñe estando despierto.

Here we find a vision of reality, like Manrique's brilliant reality of the court, as something passing and ephemeral. In Manrique it was not a dream, but almost might have been, since nothing could be constructed on it, and since it passed so rapidly that it could be compared with the morning dew which is so much like the dream of dawn. In Calderón, it is as illusory, as fleeting as something dreamed. The inference will be the same: what we see, pleasures, the beauties and greatness of this world are a deception for man. Sand and wind, woe unto him who builds on such precarious foundations, they both seem to say. Then what should one do in the face of reality?

Let us see Segismundo's solution. He outlines it by the end of the second act, in his last monologue. Yes, he says, all is a dream, every one dreams perhaps. The king dreams he is a king and dreams that he rules and commands. The rich man dreams his wealth and the poor man his trials. What is life?

What is life? 'Tis but a madness.
What is life? A thing that seems,
A mirage that falsely gleams,
Phantom joy, delusive rest,

Since life is a dream at best,
And even dreams themselves are dreams.

¿Qué es la vida? Un frenesí.
¿Qué es la vida? Una ilusión,
una sombra, una ficción.
Y el mayor bien es pequeño,
que toda la vida es sueño
y los sueños, sueños son.

So concludes the man-beast in the second act. His attitude toward the world is no longer despair as in the beginning. It is not the violent desire for beautiful realities, as in the palace. It is doubt, the tremendous doubting of real existence, the anxious questioning of the new conscience of the world. And does the truly dramatic moment of the drama arrive? What will this man, man in general, do with life, the world, with a reality of whose existence he cannot be sure, which may at best be a dream, a drop of dew as Manrique said, a blade of grass, here today to disappear tomorrow? Calderón answers the question in the third act which unfolds the work. A revolution breaks out in the kingdom of Poland as a result of which Basilio is dethroned and the people, who by now know of the existence of Segismundo, wish to crown the son in the father's place. A group of soldiers come to the tower to free him and ask him to lead them against his father. At first, Segismundo refuses to believe it is true: doubt still dominates him. And he asks those figures to leave since they are but shadows and illusions which will be blown away by the slightest breeze, like the blossom of the almond tree. He has already been disillusioned, he says, he knows now that life is a dream. What does this attitude seem to indicate? Renunciation of activity, of life itself, because of disillusionment. Since all the things we see are but passing, fleeting forms, why take part in changing or affecting them? Life is a dream: it is useless to live, to let oneself be deceived. We imagine for a moment that Segismundo will choose the attitude of withdrawal from life, from the reality in which he has so little confidence. But a few words of a soldier, completely casual, reveal to him the new course he is to take. It doesn't matter. If life is a dream let us dream, he says:

> But supposing the bright vision
> Even were true, since life is short,
> Let us dream, my soul, a little,
> Once again, remembering now
> With all forethought and prevision
> That we must once more awake
> At the better time not distant.

> *Y caso que fuese cierto,*
> *pues que la vida es tan corta,*
> *soñemos, alma, soñemos*
> *otra vez; pero ha de ser*
> *con atención y consejo*
> *de que hemos de dispertar*
> *deste gusto al mejor tiempo.*

But let us dream without ceasing to remember that some day we are to awaken. Let us bear in mind that all our power is lent and must be returned to the Giver one day. After the symbol of the dream we have here the Christian position: living or dreaming is an earthly existence;

awakening is death, the passage to another life; our power is only something lent us by God. Then Segismundo pronounces the decisive words of his life: knowing all this, let us live, and " let us boldly dare all " " *atrevámonos a todo.*" It is curious that Calderón uses the verb to dare, He means to try, to attempt everything. In Segismundo's first appearance at court, he had dared everything too; he had rushed on all that he saw and liked, guided by his unconscious and vital appetite. That was the daring of blind instinct. But now, on becoming supremely aware of what life is, after the illumination, he repeats the same word: dare. The difference is that this daring, effort, trial, is an effort of consciousness, which has plumbed the depths of life, all its illusions and deceptions, and knowing what it is, not blind as before, decides to face it, that is, to go on venturing, to go on living. In this sentence is found the whole transition of Segismundo from the savage creature of instinct to a being fully conscious. And he decides to leave the tower for the world, taking for his guide in life this thought:

> Fortune, we go forth, to reign;
> Wake me not if this is vision,
> Let me sleep not if 'tis true.
> But whichever of them is it,
> To act right is what imports me.

> *A reinar, fortuna, vamos;*
> *no me despiertes, si duermo;*
> *y si es verdad no me aduermas.*
> *Más sea verdad o sueño*
> *obrar bien es lo que importa.*

If it is real, because it is, and if it is not, for the sake of earning something when we awake.

The struggle begins and Segismundo surprises everybody by behaving with admirable sanity and moderation. He is at times tempted to give in to his instincts, as when he comes upon the woman he liked so much, but the slightest whisper in his conscience, reminding him that life may perhaps be only a dream, is enough to restore his new faith in the good and in honest action. We might say that the highest doctrine of the work, the decisive attitude of Segismundo's soul, is completely expressed in these words, when after having felt an attraction for Rosaura, he decides to renounce his desire:

> Who for human vanities
> Would forego celestial glory?
>
> *¿Quién por vanagloria humana*
> *pierde una divina gloria?*

Why should I give up divine glory for this human glory which may be but a dream? What past good is not a dream? Words almost identical with those of Jorge Manrique. All that pleasure calls beautiful turns into ashes. Let us seek the eternal, then, the true fame that ne'er reposes. What do these words mean? Simply life accepted with honor, dignity in living. And according his acts with his thought he marries Rosaura to her fiancé, and when, a little later, his father throws himself at his feet trembling and expecting punishment, he forgives him and offers him his obedience. Why does he do all this? He explains it in the last words of the work. His teacher was a dream:

Even to dream is sufficient.
For thus have come to know
That at last all human blisses
Pass and vanish as a dream.

El soñarlo sólo basta;
pues así llegué a saber
que toda la dicha humana
en fin pasa como un sueño.

One must take advantage of it while it lasts, asking for-
giveness for one's faults. And so ends the conflict of man
with the world and with himself in this magnificent
creation of Calderón.

Here the problem is much more complicated than in
Jorge Manrique, the conscience more confused, the presen-
tation much more artificial in its dramatic form; yet the
analogy with the work of Manrique is obvious. Man contemplates life within him, perceives its transitory, fleeting
character, is not even sure it is anything more than a
dream. The analysis of reality does not bring him to any
certitude about his own existence, or about the reality of
reality. The suspicion that all may be a dream will from
now on always hover over his soul. But that will not stop
him. One must boldly dare all. One must live. And one
must live actively, in acts, in good acts. For the only thing
that man can be sure of is his capacity to act well, his
power over his own acts, although these acts may be performed in the vacuum of a dream. To act well is what
matters. That is, to perform good works, to live for the
good of the conscience. Jorge Manrique's father accepted
death without hesitating, because it was the last form of

life. Segismundo accepts life even though it may be merely a dream of life. In this, precisely, is the greatness of his attitude. There is nothing heroic in accepting life when we believe it to be full of favors and delights, when we are convinced of its positive and unquestioning reality and beauty. But it is heroic to accept it like Manrique, perfectly aware that it is ephemeral and deceptive. Or like Calderón knowing that it is perhaps no more than a dream. I said in speaking of the death of Don Rodrigo: only the man that accepts the complete dimension of life, death, can be said to accept life fully. And I might add now: only he accepts life heroically who takes it, who dares all, like Segismundo, who acts, in spite of doubt and the suspicion that it may only be a dream, he, in short, who accepts dreams.

Those men who demand of reality stability, permanence, eternity are all wrong. And so also are those earthly realists mistaken, who are covetous of matter in all its forms, who believe in appearances, who exert their efforts in the attainment of triumphs of this world. But those are in error, too, who renounce life, who withdraw from the vital duty, for fear that it may pass or that it may be a dream. And this poetic attitude of our poetry seems to end with the following lesson: accept reality with all its risk of being transitory and unreal, with all its dream-like adventure. Only he who accepts death and dreams accepts life.

III

THE IDEALIZATION OF REALITY

Garcilasso de la Vega

III

At about 1530 a revolution took place in Spanish lyric poetry that was to determine definitively its course in modern times. It is usually called Italianism and many think it is merely the adoption into Castilian poetry of the eleven syllable line in its various stanza combinations. Until then, the line used in the Castilian lyric was the eight syllable line, that of the ballad. But the great transformation in our lyric can hardly be reduced to that simple external element. In reality, Castilian poetry assimilated completely the Italian Renaissance conception of the lyric, with all its metrical forms—lines and stanzas—to be sure, but with a great deal more, with its vast content of sensibility and poetic vision which had been formed in Italy from Petrarch to the sixteenth century. When we come upon a literary phenomenon of such influence and importance as the complete transformation of the lyric of a country, we are likely to consider it a spiritual phenomenon, mysterious and impossible to relate to concrete and real facts. It does indeed seem impossible to situate such a thing in time or space. It is undoubtedly a change effected by men, but under conditions which seem to have escaped all possibility of apprehension. The revolution is an historical fact, and men brought it about. But can we know any more? In other words, if we regard the new poetry as a powerful current, a great stream that will water our whole classical age, can we find its remote and hidden source? In this case, in the revolution of the

Renaissance lyric, we can, with absolute precision. The universal can be traced in the particular, and history explains how a new poetry came to Spain.

It is like a beautiful story. In 1526, the great gentleman Andrea Navagero was sent to Spain as Ambassador from the Venetian Republic. He was the perfect example of the Renaissance gentleman: a complete humanist, historian, poet, imitator of Vergil and Catullus and of the poets of the Greek Anthology, of extremely severe taste; he himself burnt many of his works before his death because he considered them inferior. Combining perfectly the ideals of the Renaissance, his love for poetry and literary perfection was comparable only to his love for nature and gardens. On visiting the gardens of the Generalife, perhaps the most beautiful in Spain, he says, after describing them: "All this grace and beauty need only someone to know and enjoy them, some man who would live there devoted to study and the suitable pleasures, without any further desire." Wonderful words, a real jewel of the spiritual harmony of the Renaissance. There was at that time, in the court of the Emperor at Granada, a young Catalan poet called Boscán, of minor importance so far as his works are concerned, but who was, as you will see, to play a very important historical role. He got to know Navagero in Granada; it is tempting to imagine the two gentlemen, Venetian and Spaniard, taking leisurely walks through the gardens of Granada, and discussing their favorite subjects, poetics, poetry. To the Spaniard, the Venetian must have seemed something of a demigod or oracle. And Navagero advised Boscán to try to write sonnets and other poems in the Italian manner in the Castilian language which he considered very suitable for those forms. Nothing more: a conversation among the myrtles of Granada, a bit of advice, that is, a seed dropped in the head of a Spanish poet.

Navagero left and soon after Boscán was obliged to leave for Barcelona too. And he tells us in a letter to the Duquesa de Soma, to whom he dedicated his second book of poems: " I left for home . . . and as I rode over the long and solitary road, meditating on various things, I often came back to what Navagero had said to me. And so I began to try this new kind of poetry." Simple and revealing words, a gem of a literary document. Let us imagine one of the long, dusty Spanish roads, lonely and desolate, a man on horseback. The journey is long, the hours pass in solitude. The horizon stretches out endlessly. The man, weary of looking at it, looks within himself. And in his head, the seed placed there by the Italian, the advice to write in our language in the new style, germinates. Boscán writes his first hendecasyllables in his mind. And so it is that on a road, thanks to its length and solitariness, the revolution in our poetry begins. Only on rare occasions (I recall only one other, at the beginning of Descartes' *Discours de la Méthode*) does history open a window for us onto a view so illuminating, so exact and yet at the same time so incredibly fantastic, in which we see the birth of a great historical event, of a spiritual revolution. Boscán begins then, from that day on, to write in the new manner. But unfortunately he was not a great poet. His attempts would never have acclimated the new current to our language if it had not been for a stroke of chance. Boscán had an intimate friend, a gentleman and poet like himself. They were a pair of perfect friends, united in life and death, in taste and ideal, as we shall see. And he encouraged and urged his friend to write poetry in the new Italianate manner too. Without that friend, the revolution would never have taken place with such amazing rapidity and success. But the friend was a man of genius, one of the greatest Spanish poets. He tried the new style, and with his genius performed this poetic miracle: that after a few years and having written only a small number of poems, he enjoyed the admiration of all and established the new poetry to this day. He was the Toledan poet, Garcilasso de la Vega. And so through this chain of circumstances, Navagero's visit to Granada, his conversation with Boscán, the latter's journey over the long and solitary road, his intimate friendship with Garcilasso, we can explain, point by point, just as the motivation of an act in a novel is explained, without missing a single link, the material circumstances of the great revolution in our lyric poetry, the detail of the mystery, as it were.

Of course, over and above these facts, be they ever so positive and well-known, mystery constantly soars, all that is inexplicable, all that is chance, what we call here genius or the marvelous poetic gift of Boscán's friend, Garcilasso de la Vega. His is not one of those novelistic lives full of adventures and exploits, but it is a life of great human plenitude, of perfect fulfillment. Garcilasso was anything but an author who wrote in the seclusion of his study, like the humanists. He is the perfect type of Renaissance gentleman. He was born in the heart of Spain, in Toledo, the most majestic and noble of all our cities. He came of noble families on both sides. Among his ancestors were some who had been writers as well as aristocrats, like the Marqués de Santillana. He must have received the humanistic education of his time, was deeply versed in Latin in which he wrote some *poèmes de circonstance*. He studied music too and it is said he was an excellent harp and guitar-player. While still very young, he entered the service of the new king, the Emperor Charles V, as a member of the royal guard. He went with the court on many of its journeys. At twenty he received his first wound in fighting for the Emperor against the rebellious *comuneros*. The following year, he takes part in a romantic expedition in defense of the Isle of Rhodes in the eastern Mediterranean. In 1525 he married Doña Elena de Zúñiga. This seems to have been a marriage of social convenience rather than a love marriage. Not a trace of conjugal love is to be found in his love poetry. The figure of his wife never appears in his lyrics. But soon after, he fell in love with a lady of the court, who was his real muse, the inspiration of his most beautiful poems as we shall see presently.

He went to Italy with the Emperor and was sent later on a secret mission to France by the Empress Isabel, which shows the favor and confidence he enjoyed in the imperial court. He lost this favor for a time through a very curious episode. A nephew of his had arranged his marriage with a lady in waiting of the Empress; the lady's parents, opposed to the marriage, secured an order from the Emperor prohibiting it. But the young people anticipated the order and were married at the Cathedral of Avila with the poet Garcilasso as their witness. The Emperor was angered by this act of disobedience and condemned the poet to confinement on an island in the Danube, close by Ratisbon. We have a reminiscence of it in one of his famous poems. From there, as a continuation of his exile, now mitigated, he went to Naples. The image of Garcilasso in Naples is perhaps the most brilliant and seductive we have of him. The Neapolitan court was then a wonderful center of literary culture and social refinement, one of those Renaissance courts in which life passes amid pleasures of the spirit and worldly courtesy and elegance. There the Spanish poet became acquainted with Italian humanists and writers. There he displayed his knowledge of Latin and Italian and poetry in both those languages and we have the testimony of many of his contemporaries in praise of his talents and his intellectual and social attractions. There is a delightful anecdote that shows us the Spanish gentleman as in an engraving of the period. It is a gathering at the home of a distinguished Italian lady, a gathering of select and subtle spirits in the luxuriant atmosphere of Naples. After sunset, when all are enjoying the marvelous twilight, some stupid and over-solicitous servants bring in the candelabras with lighted candles, destroying thus the beauty of the crepuscular half light. And the lady, whose sensibility is offended by the act, complains in the first words of a line of Petrarch: " O sorda e cieca gente," to express the lack of tact in the servants who fail to respect the nuances of twilight. And then Garcilasso finishes the complaint by ending the Petrarchan line: " a cui si fa notte innanzi sera." How revealing is this delightful detail, of a society in which sensitive souls lament over the ruin of a twilight by quoting a line from Petrarch which begins on the lips of an Italian lady and ends on those of a Spanish gentleman!

Pardoned by the emperor finally, Garcilasso returns to his service and takes part in an expedition to Tunis where he is twice wounded by lance. In the spring of 1536 he is named field marshal with three thousand men under him, and takes part in the French campaign. In passing through a place in Provence, there is a tower beside the road from which the French fire on the emperor's men. The emperor, angered, orders that the tower be taken by assault, and Garcilasso with some men rush to the ladder to scale the wall. An enormous rock is dropped from above by the defenders and wounds him so gravely in the head that he dies a few days later in Nice. He was thirty-three years old. Garcilasso himself had written:

> O finespun web, too soon
> By Death's sharp scissors clipt!
>
> *¡Oh tela delicada,*
> *antes del tiempo dada*
> *a los agudos filos de la muerte!*

As you see, Garcilasso's life was replete with human values. Like almost all of us, he carried within him two men, one visible, the other invisible. The first was the perfect courtier, the gentleman, the fighter who fulfills his duty always and dies for it. He serves his lord, goes where service calls him, and without protest or flight, obeys circumstances as life presents them and even lets himself be killed by them. Dignity, simplicity, valor, personal charm, is what we see and what all that knew him must have seen, when we review the actions of the visible man. But Garcilasso had within him an invisible man, almost always modestly hidden, answering the call not to war but to the highest peace of the spirit, the poet. He was known by people during his lifetime as a refined and cultured gentleman, to be sure, but no one knew his poetry until after his death, for out of spiritual delicacy and elegance he concealed his poems and published none during his life. His friends did know something of his poetic gift. But they did not know the true height of his creative genius, nor could they guess the importance his poetry was to have. Garcilasso was the extreme opposite of the professional poet who withdraws to the ivory tower of his spirit. His is a life open to everything; deep down in it shines that mysterious light which every poet carries, of necessity, within him, and which he concealed from people beneath the refined manners of a courtier and the valiant deeds of a soldier. Garcilasso sacrificed without hesitancy the invisible man, his secret, inner person to the visible man, the man of the world and duty.

And it seems symbolical that it should have been precisely a stone, the weight of a stone, a mass that falls by eternal physical law, that should have destroyed with all its terrible and inevitable force that delicate human soul, that marvelous instrument for the creation of inner and poetic life. The struggle between matter and spirit took place again that September day at the tower of Fréjus. And matter seemed to conquer the visible man, the emperor's soldier, the stone vanquished him. But the invisible man, the poet, was freed from all servitude and his poetic spirit triumphed over time from the very day of his death, by its creation of the most delicately immaterial poetry.

The way in which Garcilasso's works were saved is very curious too and offers us a fine example of friendship and devotion. We suppose that his family gathered together his papers and gave them to his great friend and companion in poetry, Boscán, to prepare for publication. But he died before he could complete the task. His widow, faithful to the memory of her husband and his friend succeeded in having them published in 1543. This brief and dramatic story of the works of Garcilasso is indeed moving when one considers the risk they ran of never being known. First, the poet dies without being able to have them printed. Will they be lost? No. The family collects them and gives them to Boscán; they now seem to be saved. But there is another accident, the death of Boscán. And again the danger arises that they may never be published. Thanks to the conjugal devotion of a woman, Garcilasso is saved finally and definitely from oblivion. I remember that the one time I held that first edition in my hands, I could not help thinking of the strange tricks of chance, and of how this great poetry might have been written, created and yet remained unknown. The name of Doña Ana Girón, Boscán's wife, is that of the greatest benefactress of Spanish poetry, and if in this world so many poems have been written for a woman, these at least have been saved by a woman.

The success of Garcilasso's works was immediate and complete. They were published in 1543, and before 1560 sixteen more editions of his poems had appeared, some printed in Italy, Portugal, Flanders and France. In 1574 the first learned edition appears with commentaries by the great Salamancan humanist Francisco Sánchez. Six years later another great Spanish poet, Fernando de Herrera, annotates the works of Garcilasso. That is, his poetry immediately becomes a classical text, studied and annotated, like that of a great poet of antiquity. And his name is cited as the type of poet par excellence, the model poet. But that is not as significant as the success his work attained with the poets themselves; that slight volume became the guiding star of Spanish poetry of the period. The lines of the new style he introduces, the stanzas he used, for the first time, were adopted forever more by the poets of the Spanish golden age. Poetic language and sensibility are transformed by his work as they had not been in the four preceding centuries. And so absolute was his triumph that shortly after his amorous poetry became known, religious poets used that same style, that same artistic vocabulary, those same forms to celebrate the Lord, and his greatness, and the heroic-lyric poets, like Herrera, used them to intone their songs of more epic character. It may be said that to no poet does Spanish poetry owe more than to Garcilasso. And it is wonderful to think that this beautiful and fertile work was created simply and mysteriously, like a secret game outside of his external life, without any apparent effort, as completely by divine grace, by natural gift, as the flight of a bird or the issue of a crystalline stream. There was, doubtless, great persistence, elaboration, hard work in the creation of those poems within the soul of Garcilasso as there is in the production of the stone we call the diamond. And yet the diamond appears to us in its brilliance as something so obviously beautiful, that its beauty effaces, suppresses its history. Garcilasso's poetry springs from his poetic soul with the naturalness and simplicity with which the purest glance appears in beautiful eyes, like a natural act.

Garcilasso is a poet of love. The same sentiment of melancholy and hopeless love pervades his whole work, a love that is ever aspiration and reminiscence, delicate and quivering, as though it were floating in the air and had no earthly domain on which to rest. But this love is not expressed directly, like the love of a man of his day. He adopts in his best and longest poems a very curious literary convention, much used in the Renaissance, but difficult for us to understand: the pastoral. Our literature already had some examples of this tendency in the Middle Ages, but they were merely incipient and undeveloped. From Garcilasso on, Spanish literature is invaded by countless shepherds in poetry as well as in the novel. The pastoral novel seizes the imagination of the ladies and is the rage during the sixteenth century. Two of our greatest writers do not escape this charm, the influence that the pastoral had on all minds, and each of them writes his pastoral novel. In the lyric, the eclogue will be a favorite genre for one hundred years once the example is set by Garcilasso. And it is not a little surprising to see in that century of great discoveries and innovations, of the most varied activity, in that most dynamic of centuries, how the best minds are taken with this conception of a soft, sentimental, artificial life, in which shepherds complain and discourse elegantly, with platonic reminiscences from time to time, on their amorous fortunes and misfortunes.

How can this fondness for the pastoral be understood? If we examine this tendency we see at the bottom of it one idea: nature. Bucolic poetry is supposedly nature poetry: its scene is the country; it takes pleasure in contemplating landscape; its characters are natural beings, shepherds, men who are closest to the earth. But is this nature poetry as we understand it today? There is an abyss between this nature poetry and Wordsworth. Since Romanticism, poets have tried to face nature directly, without any intermediary, have tried to let themselves be affected by it as naturally and truly as the face is by the sun and air. The men of the Renaissance took many precautions against it: one of the precautions taken against the excessive ardor and rawness of the natural is precisely the pastoral fiction. In it the two essential impulses of the Renaissance soul cross in a most interesting way. The men of the Renaissance make an apology of nature and natural forces and create almost a religion of the natural. The Renaissance justifies the universe and man. Together with the power of God, immediately after it, the power of nature is mentioned. Nature is a sort of agent of God: Cervantes, in *La Galatea*, in *Persiles* calls her " the stewardess of God." The celebrated humanist, Baltasar de

Castiglione, in *The Courtier,* tells us that " the world is a marvelous and great painting made by the hands of God and Nature." And Erasmus of Rotterdam, in the *Praise of Folly,* speaks of her as the " generator and mother of mankind." All of this reduces itself, as Americo Castro has shown in his book on Cervantes, to the conception of a Golden Age, when nature ruled over men, and made them happy, guiding them with their natural instincts which later, with the passing of time, were diverted from their right path and oppressed.

We find thus in the Renaissance soul, a permanent, positive tendency toward the natural, toward nature as source of perfection and goodness. It is the naturalistic tendency of the period, its aspect of human realism. But that force meets, conflicts with another that is in some ways opposed to it: idealism, the cult of ideas as the supreme expression of human dignity, the cultivation of the intellectual side of man, of his capacity for knowledge and abstraction. The Renaissance is essentially the cultivation of man, culture, concentration on the faculties of the mind. And on the other hand, it is also observation of natural phenomena, study of plants and animals. So that Renaissance man is inclined toward the source of the natural while he himself is not a natural being, is not a creature of nature, but a product of reflexion and the cultivation of his soul. It is comprehensible then that when his naturalistic impulse makes him turn toward the natural world, he does so with the eyes of a cultured man. Even his adoration of the natural does not spring from the contemplation of a landscape, nor from contact with the country, but comes from his intellect in the form of an idea when he tries to bring order into the world. And so we can understand, I think, the paradox that the natural, nature, in the Renaissance, is a creation of culture.

If we transfer all this to the realm of literature and poetry, the result is clear. The Renaissance poet of nature sees nature through a complicated set of reflections. Between real nature and his mind the wonderful and subtle lenses of ideas are interposed. They cannot be satisfied with the trees but only with the idea of the trees. In Renaissance landscape, delicate breezes, like ordering powers, ideas, pass through the gently swaying branches, the running brooks, the peeping birds. And thus, natural landscape is converted into an idea of itself. Having been born as a natural instinct, it rises and is raised to an esthetic category. In that way, the two tendencies that seemed to be conflicting, are resolved in a superior harmony in perfect accord with the essence of the Renaissance, and they live in peace. For me, pastoral poetry is the peace or truce between the realistic-naturalistic impulse of the Renaissance and its intellectual-spiritual impulse. And so the figure of the shepherd will no longer surprise us, nor will he seem to be an intruder or foreigner in that world. He will be, on the contrary, a character that expresses and represents it, a very important performer in that magnificent pageant we call the Renaissance. The shepherd of the eclogues is no shepherd as all the authors of eclogues well know. He is a courtier. Then why does he dress as a shepherd? Because there was in his soul a penchant for the natural, and as a complete man of the Renaissance, he gives up neither his being nor his desire to be, neither his reality as courtier nor his aspiration to be a shepherd. Can the pastoral be considered a mere disguise then? Only up to a certain point. I should say that it is not a disguise the poet rents or buys but one which he draws out from within him, which is another form, another aspect of his reality. When a poet creates a truly beautiful pastoral poem, it is because he has known how to combine art and nature in it, the two truths that dwell together in his soul. Which is what happens in the pastoral poetry of Garcilasso. For in that artificial genre, which many, imbued with positivistic criticism, have called, without further ado, false, human sentiment is expressed with a sincerity and an ardor, with a vital authenticity much greater than that of any realistic art. That is the greatest charm of Garcilasso. The Renaissance dug up marbles and adored bodies. Which did it prefer, the palpitating and perishable body or the statue? Does it choose the marble or the flesh? The Renaissance gives up neither; it is precisely the solution of that dilemma, the desire to eternalize marvelous rosy bodies of mortal flesh in the immaculate whiteness of ideas, white as marble.

That is why our poet, courtier and soldier, has left us his poetry enveloped in that pastoral fiction so characteristic of his epoch. And characteristic of Garcilasso too, for in it is seen that play of forces, that crossing of nature and ideas, harmonized in the higher unity of perfect poetry. Garcilasso was the greatest writer of love lyrics that Spain had had to that time, and still is without equal except perhaps for Bécquer. To what attitude toward reality does

this love poetry of Garcilasso correspond? What was the
reality behind his love? What is its poetry? Did he live
spiritually in an amorous world? To what extent is his
love real, to what extent poetic? Let us see.

The biographical data we have are neither abundant nor
detailed and yet it has been possible to reconstruct quite
convincingly the sentimental life which served as the
motive power of his poetical work. Garcilasso is the poet
of a single love. In spite of Keniston's opinion that there
may have been a love affair in Naples, the close study of
the poems bears out the impression of a single muse, a
single tone. In a sonnet, we first find the absolute con-
fession of his dedication to love, what we might call his
act of amorous faith and consecration. It is sonnet V,
petrarchan in tone and origin. Here he says that in his soul
is written the face of his love and all that he will write of
her in the future; she wrote it there and he does nothing
but read it. His poetry will be then only a reading of the
beauties which the spiritual contemplation of the loved
face has left in his soul. He was born only to love her, his
soul has cut her exactly to its measure, and he loves her as
the very garment of his soul. He owes to her all he has,
was born for her and will die for her:

> Lady, thy face is written in my soul,
> And whensoe'er I wish to chant thy praise,
> On that illuminated manuscript I gaze,
> Thou the sweet scribe art, I but read the scroll.
> In this dear study all my days shall roll;
> And though this book can ne'er the half receive
> Of what in thee is charming, I believe

In that I see not, and thus I see the whole,
With faith's clear eye; but I received my breath
To love thee, my ill Genius shaped the rest;
'Tis now that soul's mechanic art to love thee,
I love thee, owe thee more than I confessed;
I gained life by thee, cruel though I prove thee;
In thee I live, through thee I bleed to death.

Escrito está en mi alma vuestro gesto,
y cuanto yo escrebir de vos deseo;
vos sola lo escrebistes, yo lo leo
tan solo, que aun de vos me guardo en esto.
En esto estoy y estaré siempre puesto;
que aunque no cabe en mí cuanto en vos veo,
de tanto bien lo que no entiendo creo,
tomando ya la fe por presupuesto.
Yo no nací sino para quereros;
mi alma os ha cortado a su medida;
por hábito del alma misma os quiero.
Cuanto tengo confieso yo deberos;
por vos nací, por vos tengo la vida,
por vos he de morir y por vos muero.

Garcilasso valiantly accepts love as the central force of his life, as a complete power that envelops him from birth to death, and this love is personified in a woman whom he regards as consubstantial with his soul. The Spanish love lyric before his time, though delicate and sincere, had never attained this affirmative force, this expressive vigor. Love had been a poetic theme for ingenious arabesques, subtle thoughts. Garcilasso is certainly not the first poet to tell us he lives for love and will love unto death. Many had said it in the course of the fifteenth century. And yet, in spite of that documentary evidence, in spite of the fact that we *know* that he is not the first, something higher than mere knowledge prevails and we *feel* that he is the first. In the poets, convention and formula attenuated to such an extent their affirmation of love that we almost never feel tempted to take them seriously. But in this sonnet of Garcilasso, love breaks with a kind of persuasive ardor and convinces us of its real existence much as a fire convinces us of its reality by the heat we feel from within it. These words emit such spiritual heat that we cannot for a moment doubt the reality or potency of the flame. The other was a game; here love bursts forth, implacably, in all its seriousness. That is why I have always considered that the Spanish love lyric begins with this sonnet by Garcilasso. All that comes before it is prehistory. And its two qualities that stir us deeply are two essentially religious qualities: seriousness and fervor.

To what human being, to what muse, did Garcilasso dedicate his love and his life? We have already said that it was not to his wife, Doña Elena de Zúñiga, that the poet owed the complete revelation of love. It was to a Portuguese lady, Doña Isabel Freire, who came to the Spanish court a year after Garcilasso's marriage. The Princess Isabel of Portugal married Emperor Charles V in 1526. And when she left Portugal, it is told that she said that she could not live without the company of that lady who was to be Garcilasso's muse. So she took her with her and it was in the imperial court that Garcilasso met her. We may say that if ever women are born to be muses, certainly this woman was. Before leaving Portugal, the greatest Portuguese poet of the day, Sa de Miranda, had sung his love for her with such passion that historians say he was exiled from the court for his indiscretion. Whatever took place between her and Garcilasso? We do not know for certain, but it is entirely probable that it was a one-sided love that took hold of the poet and his poetry, but never succeeded in moving the woman who was the object of it. This passion of Garcilasso was neither accepted nor requited. The lady may have been his friend, may perhaps have accepted with pleasure his friendship, but rejected it as soon as the real love behind it became evident. The second eclogue might, it seems to me, be explained in such a way as to clarify the poet's sentimental life. In it the shepherd explains of his fortune: ever since childhood he has been the friend of a shepherdess with whom he has played in the fields and passed the most delightful hours of his life in innocent entertainment. But little by little, his friendship turns into love; and when finally one day he confesses to his intimate friend that he loves her, she flees from him and never speaks to him again. To be sure, this passage is not original; it is taken from Sannazaro, and the commentators have never suspected that it might refer to the poet. But I am inclined to believe that this is a reference to his breaking off with Doña Isabel. There can be no doubt that she was a friend of the poet and took delight in the friendship. Why does Garcilasso suddenly begin to complain of her indifference and disdain? What accounts for their separation? I think it entirely likely that what happened to the shepherd Albanio in the eclogue, his seeing himself scorned and hated by his friend when he wished to convert their friendship into a higher kind of relationship, was really what happened to the poet. The fact is that Doña Isabel married in 1529, that is, three years after her arrival at court, a gentleman called Antonio de Fonseca. The marriage was considered unequal by people, for the husband though very noble was called the fat man, and according to a chronicler of the period, had never written a line of poetry in his life. It was, in short, a match unworthy of a muse. By it Doña Isabel became a muse *déclassée*. Garcilasso expresses his grief and discouragement in many passages of his poems. All that this betrayal leaves him is a painful memory and solitude, he laments over and over again. But external life follows its course. He goes to Italy with the Emperor. And there a new and final grief awaits him: the news that Doña Isabel has died in giving birth to a child. Then it is that he probably writes his most beautiful and celebrated poem, Eclogue I, in which the voice of love rises above the note of disillusionment and bitterness, love which has this time lost its object beyond recall, forever, through death. It is the purest and clearest love elegy that has ever resounded in our language.

Such are the facts of reality, such is the sentimental story that provided the occasion for Garcilasso's best poem. As you see, the human subject-matter, the facts are not numerous or novelistic. A positivistic reasoner would find no normal correlation between what happened and the deep and lasting trace it left in Garcilasso's poetry. But we know that poets only half-live external events, or even less than half. The most transcendental events in the life of a poet are indeed based on realities of the world, begin with them, but then develop, unfold in his conscience, in his inner being, like a long drama, the first act or scenes of which only have been seen by the public, the rest of which continues invisibly toward its end, far from any possible observation by people. The poet enjoys the same privilege as the skilful Flemish lace-maker: with a thin thread, with a subtle and thin substance, she creates all of a marvelous phantasmagoria that covers a large surface with exquisite beauty. And from something which has only one dimension, the linear dimension of thread, or of facts, they draw a new reality of two or more dimensions, lace or poetry. For in the last analysis, poetry is nothing but that miracle of converting the unidimensional of brute reality into the multidimensional of spiritual creation.

Let us see finally what Garcilasso's poetic attitude was toward his amorous human reality. How did his poetry treat its reality? Let us examine the first eclogue which is, as I have already said, the pearl of all his works.

After a brief dedication, the poet presents a shepherd whom he calls Salicio, complaining softly and gently (these are the poet's adverbs) of his loved one. The lines unfold with unfailing delicacy and elegance of tone. The shepherd mentally addresses Galatea, his love, and reproaches her for her scorn which has taken from him all desire to live. She does not wish to be the mistress of a soul over which she constantly rules. The world continues its course, the stars their function, people their work, but he outside of it all, laments her forsaking him, her faithlessness. Then come the evocative words, the nostalgic questions he asks himself: What ears hear her voice now?

7

On whom has she turned her eyes now? Then the accusation of inconstancy, since she has abandoned him for another man who is unworthy of her. As you see, Salicio's poetic discourse has nothing new in it as I tell it here. What is new and exquisite is unfortunately what only a reading of the original poem can communicate: its note of tenderness and sincerity, its expressive elegance, the balance between its impassioned feeling and its terse, serene poetic surface. When Salicio ends his lamentation, another shepherd, Nemoroso, appears, offering us a variant for the preceding monologue. He complains too of being irremediably separated from his love. But now the cause of the separation is not disdain or fickleness, but death. This second part is a true love elegy.

The elegy always uses a curious psychological procedure: it longs for what is lost, dead, what can no longer be possessed in reality because death has taken it from us. But that lost good can still be redeemed or recovered in one last form: memory. If it is remembered it is not completely lost. The elegy is essentially a struggle against death, since it is the desire to revive, to give again to what we have lost the only life possible, which comes from all spiritual creation. To recall is a way of living again. But how can the poet make us feel the value of what he has lost, its immense price, which is what justifies the elegy? In one way only: by presenting it to us, evoking it to us, that is, causing to live before our eyes, by means of magic, through poetic resurrection, that which died. The elegy is is always evocation. By evoking, by recreating in his soul the image of the lost one, the poet fulfills a double function: he creates for himself the illusion of possessing, of having once more what he never again will have; and then he makes us feel the great value and loss in what has past. For that reason, evocation is indispensible to every elegy. For in that way we also have the same feeling as the poet, the feeling of loss; all that beauty is presented to us with a sharpness of outline and a power that make us imagine we can see it, touch it. Then all at once we see it disappear, vanish, die again. We too have lost something. And thus is communicated to us the very feeling sung by the poet: beauty lost.

The major part of this elegy by Garcilasso is devoted to the stirring evocation of his dead love, Elisa, whose hair he keeps in a handkerchief, weeping as he counts them one by one. This part is pervaded by sensibility of pure romantic stock, by an authenticity of feeling that takes hold of the reader, without violence however, as it passes gradually from melancholy to sadness and from sadness to despair. But the elegy does not end on a note of despair. For the poet, imbued with Renaissance Platonism, contemplates his love treading and measuring the heavens with her immortal feet. And he asks and hopes, that she may from up there hasten the wheel of time, so that he may join her in that platonic heaven, in those celestial mountains, rivers and valleys, where he will be able to rest and gather flowers with her without fear of ever losing her:

> Divine Eliza, since the sapphire sky
> Thou measurest now on angel wings, and feet
> Sandalled with immortality, oh why
> Of me forgetful? Wherefore not entreat

To hurry on the time when I shall see
The veil of mortal being rent in twain,
And smile that I am free?
In the third circle of that happy land,
Shall we not seek together, hand in hand,
Another lovelier landscape, a new plain,
Other romantic streams and mountains blue,
Fresh flowery vales, and a new shady shore,
Where I may rest, and ever in my view
Keep thee, without the terror and surprise
Of being sundered more!

Divina Elisa, pues agora el cielo
con inmortales pies pisas y mides,
y su mudanza ves, estando queda,
¿por qué de mí te olvidas, y no pides
que se apresure el tiempo en que este velo
rompa del cuerpo, y verme libre pueda,
y en la tercera rueda
contigo mano a mano
busquemos otro llano,
busquemos otros montes y otros ríos,
otros valles floridos y sombríos,
donde descanse, y siempre pueda verte
ante los ojos míos,
sin miedo y sobresalto de perderte?

The end of the poem is like a dark, dusky horizon on which a marvelous beam of dazzling light breaks: the hope of immortal life.

The relationship between this poetic matter and the human matter of Garcilasso's life is, as you see, clear. The poet sings the reality of the world, of his life. But with what attitude? How does he transform his real world into his poetic world? By a process of idealizing the reality that he himself has lived. Two shepherds appear in the eclogue, Salicio and Nemoroso. They are in reality but one protagonist, Garcilasso himself, who conceals himself behind those two names. Two loved ones are presented: the first called Galatea, the other, Elisa. And each of them is lost by each shepherd through a different cause: Galatea through marriage with someone else, and Elisa through death. Here too the poet uses his parallel method and just as he converted himself poetically into two people, he makes of his one love, Isabel Freire, two shepherdesses, two loves. And there can be no doubt that they are but one, the Portuguese lady: the lady who first scorned Garcilasso and married another man, and then died in childbirth. It is evident that the two realities are identical. In real life, a single person, Garcilasso complains of two misfortunes, scorn and death of his love. In the poem, two shepherds complain of their adversities with two women, one faithless, the other dead. How did Garcilasso pass from one reality to the other? It is perfectly obvious: by a process of idealistic dissociation. By creating from the facts given in human reality a second and higher poetic reality. There is still a third phase to this idealization. The love of Salicio and Nemoroso, which was sung to us in the first two parts of the poem as the human love of man for woman, is transformed in the last stanza into superhuman love, into the love of immortal beings that have escaped to celestial regions. And so we have been taken from material and earthly loves to the supreme conception of a platonic and divine love. From one man and one woman two lovers and loved ones were made. From a human passion divine love has been created.

Thus the poet uses the eternal forms of art to save the passing forms of live from destruction. He does not copy life or note it down. He does not accept it in its true and real form, valiantly, openly, although he knows that at bottom it may be but an illusion, a vacuum. He makes it over, idealizing it. He changes the historical fact into an ideal category with the pure art of the Renaissance. And so the poet's attitude toward reality is not that of Manrique, nor that of the Cid, but a completely new one: the projection of human events onto a higher plane; their transformation into ideas. This is a perfect example of the harmonization of the two realities: visible, transparent reality is there in Garcilasso's poem, but only as the outline of the other reality and it is the task of the spirit to strive to attain that other reality. And in the final stanza, the poet affirms his faith in that ultimate ideal reality, in that poetic heaven where she walks and where he hopes to walk one endless day, at her side, saved forever more from the fortuitous. I do not know whether these rational analyses of poetry, that I am indulging in these lectures, are of any use. But I can humbly say that when I first realized what Garcilasso's method was, his spiritual technique, as it were, I understood better what I had felt before but without being able to explain it: that marvelous alliance that is perceived throughout his poetry between a sincere sentiment, common to us all, directly human, and that impression of immateriality, of heavenliness that runs parallel to it. Like Elisa, the reader's soul walks through earthly valleys, gathers their flowers, but feels suddenly that those valleys and flowers are no longer of this world, that those flowers are no longer made of matter, that he has been transported without knowing how to a higher region, where he treads heavenly valleys and gathers unfading flowers, at the side of a love that will never leave him.

Garcilasso achieves this miracle by adopting an attitude toward reality that is not analytical or reproductive, not conformist or philosophical, but idealistic. Perhaps this world is a dream or nothing at all as Calderón and Manrique thought, but Garcilasso does not put the question to himself; what he does instead is to transform this world—which is originally ours and everyone else's—into another world, with the most magic simplicity. That is why we find in him the best example of the fusion of the two realities, and why in his poetry the most difficult of marriages is realized, the marriage of the human with the divine. And Garcilasso, human love poet, is our most divine love poet. And his attitude toward reality is perhaps the most poetic, the most essentially poetic of all. For in Garcilasso's procedure, we perceive the most pure and limpid of poetic operations: life, impure, in reality, is converted into pure poetry.

IV

THE ESCAPE FROM REALITY

Fray Luis de León

San Juan de la Cruz

IV

The sixteenth century is in the history of Spain the century of maximum action. As though impelled by a formidable inner spring, Spain rushes headlong, body and soul, toward the four cardinal points. It is the period of our great discoveries and conquests, on land and sea, from the Pacific to the Mediterranean. Spanish soldiers tread all the roads of Europe, adventurers of iron open routes to America, and these routes bear the weight of the Galleons laden with gold and of the ships that defeated the Turks in Lepanto. But for me the astounding thing is not the fact itself, not the history of Spanish action, but rather the spirit that palpitated behind it. A discovery or conquest are only external manifestations of a collective soul that seeks, that is, of a spirit that desires. What seems astounding to me is not so much what the Spaniards achieved, their material and positive conquests, which after all were soon enough submerged in nothingness. No, the astounding thing is not what they did, but what they desired. All of Spain seems to be a great will, a vehement desire, and the vision of our sixteenth century is that of a people that launches into the most tremendous of adventures, that of aspiring, of desiring without measure or end. Thus, today, in considering that period, if we look at the Andes, Naples, Tunis, that is, all the concrete forms of our action, we find a great failure. It all passed. But what is not gone is the inordinate and ardent aspiration in in the soul of a people, which found expression in those deeds, whose work was, to be sure, imperfect since it was the victim of those times, and whose powerful ideal remains reflected in our art as a pure and imperishable force. A Spanish proverb says: to desire is to be able: " querer es poder." For a hundred years in our history that was true. Spaniards could do what they desired. Later their power broke, sank into decadence. But there remains and always will be, floating over the material ruins, the memory of an immense longing, of a boundless ideal and will. So the history of Spain, which must be considered by the simple historian, sociologist or economist as an enormous failure, if felt in its pure original essence as aspiration, is poetry. And now we can understand Spanish dynamism in all its spheres. But there comes a point at which that dynamism is expressed more effectively than at others: in the spiritual life. How did Spanish dynamism manifest itself through the spiritual life?

There are many that hold, as you probably know, that Spain had no Renaissance. A German author published a work entitled " Spain, the Country without a Renaissance." Without entering here into the discussion of that question, it must be said that if intellectual activity in Spain did not express itself with the same intensity, in the same measures and forms that we usually associate with the Renaissance in other countries, that does not mean at all that Spanish spiritual life did not attain maximum proportions and heights. Spain lived its Renaissance in its own way. It refused to limit itself strictly to the purely Renaissance models although it used them all to some extent. But if there was no Renaissance in the formal and academic sense of the word, there was so great an awakening in our country in the activity of the spirit, such a rebirth of conscience in search of light, that we cannot but call it a Spanish Renaissance.

Perhaps if we recall the historical conditions of Spain at the time we shall be able to understand it better. Having recently achieved national unity, unity of conscience in one religious faith, Spain became a Catholic monarchy that served above all its religion. It fought Islam in Lepanto and Luther in Muhlberg. The religious ideal provided the tonic note of Spanish life in all its dimensions. The council of Trent, the reform of the Catholic church and the religious orders, the purification of faith and the religious life, all indicate the direction taken by our spiritual Renaissance. Now then, the religious life is the most purified expression of our spiritual preoccupation. And so we can say that in the middle of the sixteenth century in Spain religious and spiritual life are one and the same thing; and that our activity, our dynamism in thought and sensibility concentrate on the religious. The Spaniards of this period were dominated by the great problem of the soul, its existence and destiny. And so we see that while their external and material activity manifested itself in wars and discoveries, their spiritual activity expressed itself in parallel wars and discoveries in the inner realm, in formidable adventures of the soul. Our soldiers and *conquistadores* seemed to have as their motto: onward, *plus ultra.* And that desire to go further, that aspiration toward the spiritual beyond, vibrates like a flame in our literature and art.

The great captains and *conquistadores* of the inner

struggle are, to the end of the seventeenth century, the mystics. Mystical literature, in its various forms, is a real laboratory for the investigation of the activity of the soul. Santa Teresa and her companions who turn their glance inward, discover, conquer, advance through the inner realms, and try for the first time roads in the most virgin forests of the conscience. But our mystics have one remarkable characteristic. And it is that while they examine the mysteries of the spirit in the solitude and seclusion of their cells, they do not renounce the struggles of the outside world. We find in the great Spanish mystics a double being: the contemplative or visionary and the man of action. I know no more extraordinary example in history of this double personality than that of Santa Teresa, the greatest woman of action of her day, indefatigable founder of convents, who traversed all the highways of Spain in sprawling carriages, who treated innumerable people with admirable tact and diplomacy, who wrote hundreds of letters on practical questions, and who was called by a high dignitary of the church a " restless and wandering female." And on the other hand, at other times, she would pass from the reality of the outer world to the most extreme ecstacy, to a state of trance, to visions of the soul utterly detached from matter and its ends. That woman would take care of the slightest details, like, for example, the kind of bolt that should be used in the convents of her order, and then would become oblivious to all that was not union with God through rapture and transport. This peculiarity of our mystics, their realistic sense, their exact and selfless performance of the daily duties of their calling, and at the same time their prodigious capacity for detachment from the temporal, for living in the absolute, must guide us in our study of one of the highest and most original forms of our poetry, mystical poetry. The poets and poems that incarnate it are not numerous. But Spanish mystical poetry has created works of such high quality, of such great intensity, that those of profane poetry may perhaps equal it but can never surpass it. And if Garcilasso and Góngora were great poets, Fray Luis de León and San Juan de la Cruz are equal to them in perfection and greatness and superior to them in ardor and spirituality. Let us examine Spanish mystical poetry first as represented in the person and work of Fray Luis de León. Here we shall come upon an attitude toward a new reality.

Nothing conforms less to the idea of a mystic as a person withdrawn from the world, separated from its struggles, than the life of Fray Luis de León. Born in 1528, he embraced the religious life at the age of fifteen, in the order of Saint Augustine. He studied philosophy and theology at his monastery and at the University and soon began to teach in the convents of his order. In 1560 he took the degrees of licentiate and master at Salamanca and was named professor at that university the following year, a position he held to the year of his death, 1591. His was the life of a professor at the richest and most glorious Spanish university of the time. But we are wrong if we think that that position afforded Fray Luis the privilege of external tranquillity, of serenity in the course of outer events, of defense against the needs of life. Not at all, Fray Luis was almost always involved in a series of struggles, all the more painful because they arose directly out of his daily duties. The university of Salamanca was at that time a little world, divided by personal and doctrinal discord. The religious orders were almost all represented in the faculty assemblies and each one of them had a certain *esprit de corps* that caused it to regard with hostility and suspicion the members of the other orders. Every competitive examination for a chair would raise a conflict, would make the professors divide into small groups, would cause a small war to be carried on for months in that world of science. The scholastic disputes, so common at that time, contributed even more to the disunion of spirits. And still more, the differences in interpretation of theological points, so subtle and liable to error.

So that we must imagine Fray Luis, not only as the man who studies and teaches, who goes from his books to his classroom, but as a man who finds himself implicated in an infinity of little intrigues and conflicts, of wretched disputes which, though they may have begun with points of doctrine, often degenerated into simple personalities. His passionate, unequal character, at times violent, at times humble, made him even more sensitive to the wounds and shocks of that existence. To a man of delicate sensibility this continual internal discord at the University caused greater suffering than to an ordinary person. This phase of Fray Luis' existence reaches a climax when, as a result of his opinions on the interpretation of the Vulgate, hostility grows so strong against him and two other professors defending the same opinions, that the Inquisition has to intervene, and pressed by his enemies, imprisons

Fray Luis for five years. During the trial and imprisonment he remained absolutely submissive and obedient to the authority of the Church and the Inquisition and in the end he was absolved of all guilt, being ordered only to hand over a translation he had made of the " Song of Songs." It is told, and though it has not been proven historically, it is in perfect accord with his character and way of being, that when he returned before his students, he began his lecture with the following words: " As we were saying yesterday . . ." Conveying in this way that the years of confinement, adversity, injustice were effaced, eliminated from his consciousness, and that life would go on, having left him no scar, no rancor toward anyone. He held the chairs of Moral Philosophy and Bible. In 1582, he was again accused by the Dominicans of defending a doctrine in the question of grace and predestination, but this time he was not prosecuted. And so his life continues, his prestige constantly growing within his order until he is named Provincial of the Augustinians in Castile.

This is, then, what his earthly existence brought the poet: incessant work in his order, study, and an intricate network of quarrels and enmities from which he could not free himself and which culminated in the injustice of long imprisonment. Well now, the curious thing is that the poetry of Fray Luis de León is the most notable in our lyric precisely for its serene exterior, spiritual equilibrium, firm moral temper, its vision of a calm and tranquil existence. His most famous poem is " *Vida retirada* " ("*The Life Retired* ") in which he extols life in the country, the withdrawal from ambition and struggles. Anyone that read that poem without knowing anything of his life, would imagine him in platonic repose, in the shade of gentle trees, beside slow-running streams, enjoying a meditative existence without strife. How can this be explained?

Is the poetry of a great poet the reflection of his life, the more or less faithful mirror of his existence in the world? No. It is the result, the consequence of his life, over and above the facts of that life. If the poet merely recorded in his poetry what happened to him, he would not be writing poetry but history, mémoires, or a diary. He would always remain at the same level as the events. But true poetry places itself above events and though it may spring from them, it is superior to them and transports them to a plane where their contingencies are lost and only the pure essence remains. I have often thought that the number 100 is of extraordinary simplicity and beauty, with its 1 and its two zeros. But let us consider it as a sum, as the final product of a series of quantities to be added: in these quantities the other numbers alternate and vary, are superposed, until finally they laboriously add up to the final figure, which seems pure and simple to us. No one on seeing this round number, 100, thinks that it comes from the addition of many small numbers, of extremely little value, which slowly make up the final sum. Every poem is a sum, the finding of a single number, in which the rest are indeed included but no longer recognizable, raised to a single result. So the poetry of Fray Luis de León is the great product of a series of minute facts which, thanks to the patient and purifying labor of the mind, leave an impression of greatness that is in striking contrast to the trivial nature of the real things that composed it. And so we understand the attitude toward reality that his poetry reveals. Submerged in the world, placed right in the center of its passions and wretchedness, taking part in them because of the fatal law of human weakness, the Augustinian poet knew all the adversities and baseness of reality. He knew the material world and let himself be hurt by it. But not conquered. What did he do? Accept it? Idealize it? No. Let us see.

What idea in general does the poet have of this world? In the prison in which he was shut up for years, he wrote a *décima* (a 10-line stanza) in which he describes the world as " wicked." It is the harshest term he ever applied to it. In other poems he calls it a " low and dark prison." " Prison," " a deep and dark valley of solitude and tears," " tempestuous sea." He sums this impression up in a most expressive way in his famous phrase: " earthly noise." In some poems he warns us against vanity, the temptations of love, the sensuality of beauty, avarice, etc. And he condenses his warning in his question at the beginning of Ode 2 to Felipe Ruiz:

> How slender is the worth
> Of all the sun sees, whether it set or rise,
> Wealth that in India has birth
> And what the East supplies,
> Riches for which the vile throng toils and dies!

> *¿Qué vale cuanto vee*
> *do nace y do se pone el sol luciente,*
> *lo que el indio posee,*
> *lo que da el claro Oriente,*
> *con todo lo que afana la vil gente?*

His vision of the world, the world of men, their deeds, human activity, is one of disillusionment. All is vanity and error. And as for his own personal existence, there are some lines in the Ode " To Retirement " that allow us to penetrate, as though guided by a ray of light, the poet's dissatisfaction with his own life:

> Receive me in thy height,
> Receive me: from the hostile, erring host
> Of men I take my flight,
> And from vain labour lost,
> False peace by unjust sufferings ever crossed.

> *Recíbeme en tu cumbre,*
> *recíbeme, que huyo perseguido*
> *la errada muchedumbre,*
> *el trabajo perdido,*
> *la falsa paz, el mal no merecido.*

Here we see all the spiritual anguish and torment of Fray Luis. For if in his general judgments on the world we may find something of the commonplaces said by the Catholic concerning this valley of tears, here we see the conscience of a man dissatisfied with himself in this life of reality. " Labour lost " means that Fray Luis de León, great worker, tireless student, ends by believing that effort is useless. " False peace " means that the repose we find here is really only apparent, erroneous. " Unjust sufferings " are the injustice, the wounds inflicted on his honorable soul through the stupidity and passion of men. All the bitterness and weariness of the professor of Salamanca, who was obliged to struggle daily, to quarrel with his colleagues, to see himself accused and imprisoned, to find in the brief moments of repose only an apparent and false peace, throbs here with the deep note of a human complaint. It is man complaining about the reality of the world that surrounds him, no longer the moralist or priest thinking about the vanity of all things. His lines are more confessional, more confidential, for they are the expression of one of those moments of weakness when the soul speaks without dissimulation.

That is his vision, his feeling about reality. What to do about it? Fray Luis' solution has, we might say, two degrees or phases. Fray Luis has been considered one of our most important nature poets because of his poem "The Life Retired," in which he sings the delights of his garden that really existed and which he celebrates again in his prose work " The names of Christ." It has been said that this poem in its feeling for nature accords with the Horation conception, and literally that is true. But when this poem is seen together with the other works of the poet, it becomes evident that he ascribes value to nature, not so much in and for itself, but for its capacity to offer refuge, peace, comfort to a soul that is weary of the world. In the evils of this world there is one single exception: the country, its simple and peaceful lesson. This point of view is confirmed in the ode " To Retirement." There nature is called a " sure port," " happy, gentle repose," and the poet asks the mountains to carry him to their heights, far from men, so that he may be free from their poison:

> At last, O thou serene retreat
> From all my wanderings! Thou balm desired
> So long, that bringst me healing sweet

From wounds naught else can heal! Inspired
Seclusion, gracious welcome for the tired!

¡Oh ya seguro puerto
de mi tan luengo error! Oh deseado
para reparo cierto
del grave mal pasado!
Reposo alegre, dulce, reposado!

The first phase then in Fray Luis' attitude toward reality
might be called retirement, withdrawal, separation from
men, and refuge in the goodness of Nature. But even
more than withdrawal, on one occasion the poet calls it
flight and gives this advice to a friend: " Flee, for only he
who flees, escapes." We have here the extreme point in
the position of separation and retirement: flight, escape
from the world. In this respect the poetry of Fray Luis
might be said to approach classical poetry which distinguishes two things within reality: one, men, their miseries
and meanness, the other, clear and lustrous nature that
purifies everything. Man in this case only flees from one
zone of the real, the human, that created by men, but he
nevertheless remains in another zone, also of reality, the
world of nature. His flight is a flight within the same
level, within the same plane of the earth, from cities to
the country, from earthly noise to natural serenity and
solitude. Fray Luis who translated Horace does at times
adopt this attitude. But in him, the desire for flight is not
simply the desire of the epicure for a delicate, material
peace, no, it is not the pagan ideal. Fray Luis is a mystic.
And if there is in flight, in escape, a negative attitude, that
of purely and simply denying oneself to the world, we see

the great lyrical inspiration of our poet convert it into a positive aspiration, that is, flight toward an end or objective. And that is what is characteristic of his escape, his manner of escape, we might say. Why, to what end does he escape? In flight there is an attitude that is to some extent cowardly: one flees to free oneself from something, or at least, to avoid suffering. But the attitude of Fray Luis is very different: it is not for the sake of freeing himself from suffering, but out of the incompatibility of his soul with the world, out of a sort of delicacy and sensibility that make all that surrounds him seem repugnant to him. And above all, what is typical of the evasive attitude of the poet is that he flees *from* something, to be sure, but *toward* something.

How does Fray Luis flee and whither does he flee? Anyone who has read his poems closely must have noticed the mysterious sensation of flying they give: he does not flee by walking or running, no indeed. The poetry of Fray Luis soars; his stanzas have a wonderful lightness and ascensional power. In certain poems, like "Serene Night," "To Music," "To Felipe Ruiz," that ascensional effect is so clear that we seem at the end of each stanza to rise one plane higher. That is, we are not only transported, but we can actually perceive that elevating power at various distances from the earth. His lines abound in words expressing soaring, ascending, cleaving the air, taking flight, going beyond. Take the most perfect example at the end of the "Ode to Felipe Ruiz" (On Constancy and Moderation):

The chain that bound me, see
Burning to make me prisoner, thou hast riven:
I fly aloft through thee
Comfort thy wrong has given,
So that I freely tread the floor of heaven.

Rompiste mi cadena
ardiendo por prenderme; al gran consuelo
subido he por tu pena;
ya suelto encumbro el vuelo,
traspaso sobre el aire, huello el cielo.

And naturally the goal of that journey, the port of that
escape, cannot be any other for a Spanish mystic than
heaven. Fray Luis' poetry is poetry of the celestial. In
one poem, Heavenly Life describes celestial existence to
us, with God tending the flock of the happy souls saved.
On hearing his blind friend Salinas play music, the poet's
soul is transported to a heavenly region, " sea of sweetness," where the soul is submerged, free from strange or
accidental sounds, in mystical rapture and ecstasy:

Through sea of melody
In rapture sweet the soul doth onward glide,
And sinks there finally,
Until whate'er betide
Beyond it to its senses is denied.

Aquí la alma navega
por un mar de dulzura, y finalmente
en él así se anega,
que ningún accidente
extraño o peregrino oye o siente.

On gazing at the heavens on a serene night he is exalted

as he thinks of the wealth hidden behind its starry surface.
"Awaken, mortals," he says:

> O skyward lift your eyes,
> Unto this heavenly eternal sphere!
>
> *Ay! levantad los ojos*
> *a aquesta eterna celestial esfera!*

For Fray Luis, heaven is no vague place. He conveys first
one dominant sensation: light. "A pure, free, happy day,
I ask." "Temple of clarity," "unsullied light," "radiant
pure light that never dims," "resplendent light," "eternal
fire of light." Fray Luis expresses the heavenly with these
words. In his lines a most brilliant light shines. There
are no colors, no chromatic effects, only this sensation of
pure luminosity.

Heaven is light. But beside that, heaven is the revelation
of truth, the explanation of the universe. Fray Luis was a
platonist, and for him heaven is the kingdom of ideas and
pure spirits. In his poetry the Christian ideal and platonic
clarity form an ideal world that is unequaled in our lyric.
We said luminosity, light. This is the impression of the
senses. But we would add now: clarity, that is, the light
of the intelligence. The luminous in him has two phases:
seeing and understanding. Heaven is supreme light and
supreme intelligence. The joy of the soul is to be saved
in the comprehension of the world, which from below
could not be understood, was all confusion. Two poems
express this to us, the "Ode to Music" and "Ode I to
Felipe Ruiz." Transported by music to heaven he hears
up there the original source of all music which, he says, is

composed of concordant numbers that form a sentence that is then echoed in sweet harmony from the music created on the earth:

> The great Master there it sees,
> His hand upon the mighty lyre, with train
> Of skilful cadences,
> Create the holy strain
> That this eternal temple doth sustain.

> And since in sweet consent
> Those numbers flow symphonious, reply
> Concordant is soon sent,
> And both together vie
> In a mixed power of softest harmony.

> *Ve cómo el gran Maestro*
> *a aquesta inmensa cítara aplicado,*
> *con movimiento diestro*
> *produce el són sagrado*
> *con que este eterno templo es sustentado.*

> *Y como está compuesta*
> *de números concordes, luego envía*
> *consonante respuesta,*
> *y entrambas, a porfía,*
> *mezclan una dulcísima harmonía.*

You see that this vision is expressed entirely in platonic terms. Fray Luis was a mystic, to be sure, but a mystic of order, of the numbers of harmony, a mystic saturated with classical and platonic substance. And in the other poem he dreams that he arrives at heaven, not to rest, but to see. What does he see? All that is and all that has been, the essential hidden principle of all things:

In my new life elate,
Converted into light of radiant sheen,
At one and separate,
What is and what hath been
Shall I see and its true origin unseen.

Allí a mi vida junto
en luz resplandeciente convertido,
veré distinto y junto
lo que es y lo que ha sido,
y su principio propio y escondido.

How significant these words are! It is the vehement desire of the philosopher, the desire for truth, the eagerness to reach the principle of all things. He will see, he says, the pillars that prop the earth, the cause of earthquakes, the source of all fountains, the place where lightning starts and where God stores the snow. He will see who directs and illuminates the stars. He will see where eternal light and fire originate and are kept. And finally, the mansions of joy, made of gold and light, where the blessed spirits dwell:

Yea, in the highest sphere
Those dwellings of delight shall I behold:
Motionless they appear,
Fashioned of light and gold,
The mansions that the spirits blest enfold.

Veré sin movimiento
en la más alta esfera las moradas
del gozo y del contento,
de oro y de luz labradas,
de espíritus dichosos habitadas.

Here, in this pristine and resplendent world, the flight of

Fray Luis ends. His flight was not an escape, as it may have seemed in the beginning, but a search. And two persons escape on this flight: one, the sensitive, hurt man, the Christian, suffering from the miseries of the world which is a jail or prison, persuaded of the vanities of this reality. But the other is the spirit that anxiously seeks an understanding of the terrestrial sphere. The first escapes from the reality of envy, evil, suffering; the second, from confusion, error, darkness. And for that reason, we see Fray Luis ascend by means of two instruments of flight, of two impelling forces, of the two most perfect wings: the longing for peace, moral light, tranquillity of the soul and freedom from its mortal limitations, is one of them. And the other is thirst for knowledge, the ardent desire to understand the world from above, in all its order, harmony and principle. Flight of the mystic and platonist, of the senses and intelligence, marvelous fusion in that poet of the two sixteenth century ideals: Renaissance clarity, the desire to comprehend the world through ideas, and the mystical impulse to ascend to a higher world through union with the divine. Those are the why and whither of the escape from reality in this great poet.

The highest and most inflamed Spanish mystical poetry was to spring from the soul of another monk, that of San Juan de la Cruz. He was born in 1542 of a very humble family. His mother was left a widow while he was still a child, and they moved to Medina del Campo which was then a very rich city, an important commercial center. There he attended a Jesuit school and it may be assumed that he knew very well one of the books of greatest importance, in that century, in the formation of religious spirits, the famous *Exercises* of Saint Ignatius of Loyola. But at the same time he became a nurse in a hospital. We see him then from his early youth near the sick and suffering, in close contact with the physical miseries of humanity, helping as he could, materially, and we may well suppose, spiritually, to alleviate them. But one day he has a vision, or rather he hears while he is praying what seems to him to be an order from God: "You must serve me in a religious order which you will help to restore to its former perfection." And he enters the Carmelite Order, that of Santa Teresa. He does not undertake his work of reform at once but goes first to Salamanca for four years and studies at the same university in which the other great poet, Fray Luis de León, was professor, and during the very years that he taught there. We do not know whether he ever attended his classes, but our imagination cannot resist seeing this young friar, of slight stature, who carried within him the soul of an extraordinary poet, seated on one of the hard wooden benches in one of the dark lecture-halls of that house of science, listening to the words of that professor, of that other great poet of the spiritual life, in one of those corners that seem like the chosen and sacred places in world history. It was during those years at Salamanca, his biographers assume, especially Baruzi, and rightly so, that the friar received what we might call his literary education which in large part made possible the realization of his poetic work. Isn't it entirely likely that at that time, apart from his religious reading, there fell into his hands the poems of Garcilasso which he undoubtedly knew, and other profane works like *The Courtier* of Castiglione, in which the theory of platonic love is so wonderfully explained, and even Petrarch's treatise on the solitary life, translated by then into Castilian? His life in Salamanca was utterly austere, and it cannot be imagined that the cultivation of letters, of profane knowledge, in any way tempted him to give up his inner vocation; it was only a marginal or secondary acquisition which he stored away unconsciously for the service of his inner purpose at a future day.

The year 1567 is decisive in his life, for it is then that his meeting with Santa Teresa takes place. From the first moment, she sees in San Juan a wonderful means of undertaking a reform of the monasteries analogous to the reform she had been carrying out in the convents. And those two exceptional souls, of unique temper, form from then on a couple, one of those couples united by no earthly love, nor as person to person, but by communion in the same ideal. The spirit of San Juan, full of secret ardor, burned with the longing to serve God; his meeting with Santa Teresa was like a spark that kindled his soul, in which such power to burn, to consume itself was shut up. History tells of battles, of meetings between statesmen. If an external history of the spiritual life of humanity were ever to be told, this meeting of San Juan and Santa Teresa, so rich in consequences, would be one of its essential moments. San Juan from then on devotes himself, body and soul to the work of reform. But this reform aroused tremendous opposition in the other branch of the Carmelite Order, the calced, who fought against the discalced,

had the support of ecclesiastical authorities and caused
Santa Teresa so many misfortunes. For San Juan, too, the
hour of the most cruel suffering comes: authorities order
the new reformed convents closed. And the friars who
accomplished and defended the reform were ordered imprisoned. One evening men appear at the house where
San Juan lives, break down the doors of the cells, and
carry off the monks, prisoners. San Juan, unable to put
out of the way or destroy some of the papers in which the
plans of reform are discussed, swallows them.

He is imprisoned in Toledo, in a narrow and dark cell.
The room had a tiny loophole way up near the ceiling,
so that when San Juan needed to use his prayer book, he
would have to stand on a stone in order to get near the
light—so little light was there in the room. Can't we see
a wonderful symbol in this moment in San Juan's life, as
we imagine him standing, exerting himself to reach the
thin ray of light coming from heaven? Can't we see his
soul, confined in its darkness and prison, never resigned
to them, as it gazes at the light which it cannot reach, as it
straightens itself out, stretches as much as possible in order
to take in some of its brightness? His life could not have
been harder, more bitter. From time to time he would be
taken down to the refectory and chastised there before all
the monks, but he accepted it all with the greatest humility
and patience. And it was in that terrible period of solitude
and desolation that he began to compose his first mystical
verses. And he saw himself subjected to one of the most
horrible tortures conceivable, that of not being able to
write them down because he had no ink or paper. Once—

there is documentary evidence for this—he asked his jailer to do him the charity of bringing him ink and paper so that he might write down a few lines of devotion. But he carried most of his verses in his memory. Can you imagine a greater spiritual martyrdom than this, feeling the living forms of poetic thought born within you and having no way of setting them down? In that cell in Toledo one of the most frightful human dramas was enacted for we know not how long. Nor is it possible to conceive a strength and greatness comparable, an endurance equal to those of that man who preserved, engraved in his memory day by day, what God inspired in him and what men would not let him keep. If the drama was terrible, the triumph of San Juan over all and over his own weakness was miraculous. In the meantime from without, Santa Teresa and her friends made every effort to obtain his freedom. But since they could not secure it, San Juan finally succeeded in escaping from his prison one night, after five years of imprisonment, and in reaching a safe place.

How did he leave? Broken, conquered? Quite the contrary, inflamed with a new strength and ardor for his work. After the conflict with the calced Carmelites, his enemies, calms down, he is able to devote himself to the founding of monasteries of the new discalced rule. This is a period of tremendous external activity. He goes from monastery to monastery, travels incessantly, confesses nuns, exhorts and encourages his companions in religion, he is, in short, a living and inexhaustible force, that takes delight in serving his cause. And there is every reason to believe that it is in this period of his great activity as founder that one must place also his activity as mystical writer, that it is in the brief periods of rest that his calling allows him that his written works begin to take form, his poems and prose treatises which commentate them. At this time San Juan resides in Andalusia much of the time, and some of it in Granada, the city of the marvelous gardens. If the period of suffering and hardships was spent in dry and harsh Castile, it seems that God wanted to place this other period of relative peace and serenity in the most beautiful and gentle part of Spain, in Andalusia.

The last months of his life were bitter once more because the Prior of his Order made him go to the city of Ubeda and persecuted him with constant admonitions and rigors, even during his painful illness. But he accepted it all and told a companion that he had always asked God to give him Purgatory in this life. One day, another friar, on seeing him so ill, went in search of the three best musicians in the city, brought them to his cell, and had them sing in order to provide some kind of comfort for his soul. The document says that "they did it very well," but the Saint asked them to stop, had them fed, and refused to listen to them, affirming that "it was not right that the suffering sent him by God should be diverted with music." He was sure that he would know when his last moment came and promised his friends to let them know in time. At eleven thirty, he called them to his bedside. At twelve he died, on the fourteenth day of December, 1591, five months after the death of the other great mystical poet of whom we spoke, Fray Luis de León.

The work of San Juan de la Cruz is in the highest degree mystical. It includes several treatises in prose, each of which is a long commentary on the poem that precedes it and summarizes a mystical doctrine. So that the number of San Juan's important poems can be said to be no greater than half a dozen, and of these only three are absolutely essential. But each one of them is an extremely intense condensation, a highly powerful extract, of all the poetic intuitions of the author. They give an impression of being charged with poetic potency like no other work written in this world, and that is not surprising since all of a very active and deep spiritual life went into the perfecting and illuminating of three or four poems, three or four visions. Let us say at once that the attitude of San Juan in his poetry is essentially that of escape; his is an example of the most tenacious and laboured escape conceivable. All of his poetry is the substitution of the realities of the spiritual life for those of the world. He replaces reality with a vision. But the vision is presented by means of symbols that the poet takes from material life, so that this poetry, while being an escape from the real, uses symbols of profound material reality. The soul that seeks is the lover, and God whom it seeks is the Beloved, as in the " Song of Songs." The place where they meet is like the scene of a divine, nocturnal pastoral, one of those creations of the human imagination, in which the eyes think they recognize sensible appearances, trees, animals, things, while the spirit trembles on perceiving that they are mere signs for invisible and bodiless values. That is why San Juan's poetry produces the strangest sensation of unreal reality, or of

real unreality. We feel disconcerted as if, on the one hand
we were still on this earth which we had not abandoned,
but on the other, were transported to a superhuman world.
Is that world that San Juan describes familiar or foreign
to us?

It is the world of symbols. A familiar world, up to a
certain point, because the symbolical element is the same
as that used by the profane bucolic poets, namely, valleys,
rivers, animals, shepherds. But it is at the same time very
strange, for it is transformed into a pure inner world, the
world of the conscience. When he writes: " Oh living
flame of love " the reader feels all the heat of a real flame,
that burns and consumes. Now we think that we have
seized, apprehended a reality, that of fire. But when three
lines below he tells us how delicately that flame touches
him, how gently it burns, we feel that we have seized nothing, that the poet has shown us for a moment a fiction of
reality only to flee from it at once toward a dark and symbolical meaning of the spirit. It is not a procedure that
renounces the presence of sensible reality by shutting itself
up in the purely conceptual world of other mystics. Reality
is always present in his work, and in the " Spiritual Canticle," there are lines that give us the most exquisite and
delicate picture in our language of the beauties of rustic
life and in them we perceive the breezes, fragrance, forms
of the outer world. What San Juan does is to penetrate
these apparent realities, immerse himself in them, pierce
their outer covering, and then, after using them as instruments for spiritual search, convert them into symbols of
something mysterious and obscure. His technique is that

of immersion or penetration, like that of the diver or miner. The reader takes pleasure in the contemplation and enjoyment of the material world that San Juan creates in his verses with incomparable sensual power and plastic force but no sooner has he begun to enjoy it than he feels himself violently pushed, dragged toward the hidden meanings which all that has for the poet's soul; and from the external life that was presented to him, he sees himself transported to an unknown and fantastic world of the spirit.

And what is San Juan's way of escape? It may be reduced to the one word " night." San Juan is the poet of night. But the night which he, like no one else, has described lyrically in the " Spiritual Canticle," in five lines, is a symbol. It is a great symbol, the favorite symbol of his soul. Let us examine the poem entitled " Dark night of the Soul." It is a dark night, San Juan says. The soul, inflamed with love, goes out without being seen by anyone, when the house is already at rest (the house at rest means the spirit freed from all earthly passion and impurity) :

> Upon an obscure night
> Fevered with love in love's anxiety
> (O hapless-happy night!)
> I went, none seeing me,
> Forth from my house where all things quiet be.

> *En una noche oscura*
> *con ansias en amores inflamada,*
> *¡oh dichosa ventura!*
> *salí sin ser notada,*
> *estando ya mi casa sosegada.*

In the dark (the poet insists on the note of obscurity) it goes up a secret ladder. It looks at nothing, sees nothing. What light guides it then?

> Without a light or guide,
> Save that which in my heart burnt in my side.
>
> *Sin otra luz y guía*
> *sino la que en el corazón ardía.*

A light from within, an ardor of his own is what the poet contrasts with the darkness of others, with the darkness of night. But it happens that this darkness of the night is the guide that directs him; the poet is led by obscurity itself and in this way arrives at the loved one, God, and rests in him. He tells us that the light of night permits him to see more clearly than that of noon:

> That light did lead me on,
> More surely than the shining of noontide.
>
> *Aquesta me guiaba*
> *más cierto que la luz del mediodía.*

What is the effect of this strange atmosphere, of this singular night? A sensation of obscurity, to be sure, but of an obscurity that helps one to see, that directs the soul to its Love, God. And also a marvelous impression of mystery, but what I should call translucent mystery, almost transparent mystery. There is no more mysterious poetry in our language than that of San Juan, but at the same time, none more revealing, none less confused or uncertain. In another poem we find the same curious effect of obtaining the sensation of light in the soul by accumulating the elements of darkness in the night. Even the technical device, the refrain, reveals an obsession with night. It is the " Song of the soul that rejoices in knowing God through Faith." " Cantar del alma que se huelga de conoscer a Dios por fe." The poet speaks of a mysterious fountain " that spurts and runs " and does not cease to spurt and run, " aunque es de noche," " although it is night ":

> *Aquella eterna fonte está ascondida,*
> *que bien sé yo do tiene su manida*
>   *aunque es de noche.*
>
> *Su origen no lo sé, pues no lo tiene,*
> *mas sé que todo origen de ella viene,*
>   *aunque es de noche.*
>
> *Sé que no puede ser cosa tan bella,*
> *y que cielos y tierra beben de ella,*
>   *aunque es de noche.*

This sentence " although 'tis night " is repeated every third line. The fountain is deeply hidden, but he knows whence it springs, " although 'tis night." He does not know what its original source is, for it has none, " although 'tis night." But it is the most beautiful in the world, there is no other so beautiful in heaven or earth, and the poet knows it " though 'tis night ":

> *Que bien sé yo la fonte que mana y corre,*
>   *aunque es de noche.*

By the end of the poem, the power of this short refrain, constantly repeated, is so great, that the spirit of the reader lives in an atmosphere of night, created by the poem, for which night is its very air. It is night: this impression imposes itself first but it is not the only one. For the final effect is not night, really, darkness, not-seeing, by any means. It is seeing in spite of the night, through the night, although it is night. The " although," *aunque,* rises above the *night.* And the result is that there is created, by a kind of poetic miracle, a sensation of darkness which instead of being negative, of preventing one from seeing, is positive, helps one to see, and does not obliterate the seeing of the soul, the marvelous inner vision. It is the revelation of light through darkness.

And here we come upon the very core of San Juan's system of escape: it is one of negations, renunciations, bareness. Let us see how. How does one reach the goal of life, union with God? In the poem of the dark night, when the soul, the lover, finds her Beloved, she has him lie on her breast and sleep. All is quiet and calm. The senses are suspended, he says. That is, material life has been annihilated and sight, touch, hearing do not function. Life stops:

> . . . .
> And in my body all my senses died.
> All things I then forgot,
> My cheek on Him who for my coming came;
> All ceased, and I was not,
> Leaving my cares and shame,
> Among the lilies and forgetting them.

> . . . .
> *y todos mis sentidos suspendía.*
> *Quedéme y olvidéme*
> *el rostro recliné sobre el Amado,*
> *cesó todo y dejéme,*
> *dejando mi cuidado*
> *entre las azucenas olvidado.*

And for the purpose of indicating the desired end of the joy of the soul, the poet uses a verb: to forget. " I forgot." He means that in the denial or material existence, in the suppression and cessation of all that is real, in the surrender of oneself, is where one finds the highest joy, the ultimate form of life. The poet has created something that is almost a void, has created a solitude around his earthly being, for God. And why? Is the void an end in itself? Not at all. Let us consider what he says in an aphorism: " The immense good of God can find place only in an empty and solitary heart." That is, supreme plenitude will be obtained only by dint of this labor of renouncing and of emptying oneself. Thus, the constant immersion in obscurity, in darkness. For only by denying oneself to light, depriving oneself of light, does one conquer the supreme light of the soul. We see, then, that this procedure and symbol of the night express to perfection his attitude toward reality.

The poet expresses it conceptually in other works of his. In one of his poems, he speaks of " An understanding by not understanding, a knowing by not knowing, so high that learned men will never be able to understand it." That is, understanding attained through not understanding; an affirmative result, knowing, reached by a negative course, not knowing. A procedure then of renunciation for greater conquest. He writes in an aphorism: " Renounce thy desires and thou shalt find what thy heart desires." So that the task of the soul and of poetry will be the creation of an immense, dark solitude, at the end of which are to be found unique light and company. One must escape, flee from all worldly reality, from all human desire, precisely in order to find the objective of the soul. The poet expresses this in another sentence in the Ascent of Mount Carmel: " In order to come to know everything, do not wish to know anything at all. In order to come to possess everything, do not desire to possess anything at all." The doctrine, then, of bareness, of detachment, of renunciation, as the way to the highest possession and wealth. Translating this into poetic terms we might say: " in order to arrive at seeing all, pass over the realities of the world of things, do not wish to see anything of this earthly life." And so this poetry seems to us a prodigious flight over the beauties of the world, its perfumes and presences, a flight in which the poet passes through them, thrusts them from himself, in order that, after drenching himself in darkness, he may remain facing the supreme light.

These are the two methods of escape used by the two greatest mystical poets of Spain. I might call the method of Fray Luis centrifugal, since he extended himself toward the heavens, flying, rising upward. And that of San Juan centripetal, for he submerged himself more and more deeply inward, downward. Poets of vertical spirituality, and not realistic horizontality, each of them seeks his spiritual and poetic world along one road. Much has been said of the inner life, of the reality of the soul superposing itself upon the reality of man and things. I do not know of any other case of escape, of flight toward the inner life, like that of San Juan. Fray Luis de León dreamed of brilliant worlds, expressed in forms that still referred more or less to outer realities. San Juan renounces all this and escapes into his soul. And after all, his escape is the greatest escape man has ever accomplished on this earthly surface, so full of beauties for our human senses, toward the mine of the soul, immeasurably dark and at the same time incomparably luminous, and in whose depths are found beauties far higher than all these that we touch with our hands of flesh or see with our mortal eyes.

V

THE EXALTATION OF REALITY

Luis de Góngora

V

The Italianate type of poetry, which we saw was introduced by Garcilasso at the beginning of the sixteenth century, prevailed for many years and was indeed the only Spanish poetical school. The mystics, as well as the profane poets, were faithful, each in his own way, and in accordance with his subject-matter, to the poetic norms of the Renaissance. But early in the seventeenth century something happens which is equivalent to a new poetic revolution in our literary history, something which alters the relatively peaceful course of our lyric. This event is one of those that might be called explosive. It falls in the midst of the spiritual life like a bomb, violent and full of expansive force; it agitates all the strata of the air, its flash and thunder rise above all that is ordinary and start a whirlwind that will not be calmed for a long time to come.

The event is the publication of two poems by Luis de Góngora, the *Soledades* and *Fábula de Polifemo y Galatea*. With these a new poetry, a new literary school, is established, *cultismo* (cultivated obscurity of style), which derives some of its elements from the Italian and carries them to their final, most extreme consequences. *Cultismo,* the poetry of Góngora, is a poetry of extremes. I don't think it can be better defined. Góngora is the perfect example of the nonconformist, the exceptional artist who arouses through his work the greatest antipathies and the most ardent admiration, who stimulates discussions and polemics; he is the true agitator of the whole period.

A question arises with regard to his poems that is still vital and significant today: the intelligibility of poetry. Critics and public have often asked: has the poet the right to write poetry that is not easily and directly intelligible to all? Should he so rise above common understanding as to convert his work into a kind of spiritual enigma, for the solution of which the effort ordinarily expended in reading is insufficient? If this question was important in the seventeenth century, it is more and more so today. Throughout the nineteenth century, a battle rages between what I might call the rights of the poet and the rights of the public. The modern artist, especially since Romanticism, has been asserting with ever greater ardor his personality, his privileges of spiritual individuality. That individuality or personality has become a sort of egotism. The artist is oblivious to the rest of the world, has created a language of his own out of ordinary language, dispensing with the usual norms of everyday speech. It is no longer a question of a poetic or literary language as distinct from daily, ordinary language, for this distinction has always existed, and in the sixteenth as well as in the eighteenth century, the language used by poets and merchants, for example, was completely different. No. At that time poetic language had its special character, was, as it were, a class heritage, but it was collective. And what the modern artist in many cases has tried to do is to individualize literary language by escaping from every accepted norm for the sake of originality and novelty; it was inevitable that he should run up against all that is usual, common, accepted in language. The modern artist eager to find and express his personality, has attempted to do so very often by means of language; to express a new personality has been for him an attempt to speak poetically in a new language. But the conflict arises because while the artist has become more anxious to express his individual self, the public has grown more conscious of its formidable collective self and is trying more and more to impose its vast anonymous personality. This phenomenon is seen in romanticism, that is, at the end of the eighteenth century. The Age of Enlightenment, in its effort to bring knowledge to everyone, gave birth to that myriad-headed monster called "the public." And using this metaphor further, we might define the conflict as a battle between one head, that of the artist and the hundred thousand or million heads of the monster public. If the artist has rights, the public seems to say, so have I: he writes for me. He should write for me. And what does the public demand? Simply to understand. There must be a fallacy here, a great misapprehension. For if the public wishes to understand, the poet in his turn, wants to be understood. Is this all then nothing but a game, a game of hide-and-seek, in which the two seeking each other, hide from each other? No. The term understanding is very vague. The average man today is taught, or rather the attempt is made in school to teach him to understand. His logical and rational faculties are developed. And when he thinks he has acquired the ability to comprehend quite perfectly, he tries to read a poem by Coventry Patmore or Stéphane Mallarmé and finds that he understands nothing or almost nothing. Then he rises in revolt against the artist, impelled by a feeling, in part justifiable, of resentment and annoyance. And with his hundred thousand heads, he asserts his rights demanding that those who write, write clearly, so that he may understand them. And by this simple act, the artist finds himself rejected by, excluded from the circle of the public.

I have always thought that if a poet is extravagant it is because the attitude of the public has made him extravagant. If things seem strange, it is often only because they are insufficiently understood. And the problem is even more critical today, since the public that has been flattered and narcotized by so many pseudo-artistic products refuses to make an effort to understand. A kind of indolence, a deep lack of attentiveness is the most serious illness of the modern spirit. There are so many things that demand one's attention that one ends by giving it to no one of them. Museums and cheap books add enormously to this lack of attention. And since, on the other hand, the poet is an ever more complicated being, of increasing spiritual complexity, with more and more to communicate, the conflict is intensified. The poet requires more attention than ever, more effort than ever; and the public exerts less than ever. What hope is there? I recall a wonderful sentence of Proust: "The last quartets of Beethoven created the public, that had never existed before, for the last quartets of Beethoven." The hope is that the new art may create its own public, that it may win zones of good will and intelligence in the vast anonymous mass of the general public. Fortunately the poet is never alone. If he has not the following of the great numbers that read the politician or facile essayist, he always has a group behind him, the group that he has created with his own gift of communication. Please excuse this digression but it will perhaps serve as a setting for the problem involved in the poetry of Góngora.

Góngora is one of those poets that are called obscure, difficult, incomprehensible. Rightly so, as we shall see. His life was in no way extraordinary insofar as its human course was concerned. He was born at Cordova. He studied at Salamanca about the same time as Fray Luis de León. Then he held a prebend at the Cathedral of Cordova. From his early youth he wrote poems, many of them jocular and gay, that attracted much attention. But he was for a time only one poet among many. His personality had not yet completely revealed itself. In the year 1612 his two longest and most important poems, *Polifemo* and *Soledades*, became known to the public. It would be difficult to imagine anything more amusing than the battle waged in the literary world as a result of those two poems. All writers were divided into two absolutely irreconcilable camps. Around Góngora's work there sprang up, like a luxuriant growth of ivy, a whole literature of commentaries, attacks and defenses. We can scarcely conceive today the ferocity and violence of literary life in our seventeenth century. Two great writers, Lope de Vega and Quevedo, were passionate literary enemies of Góngora. On every possible occasion, both camps exchanged the lowest and most brutal insults in words so disparaging and offensive that most people would be embarrassed to pronounce them today. But this was only a colorful aspect of

10

the great polemic. Góngora's work raised the question of difficulty and obscurity in poetry. Some friends defended him ardently. Others wrote commentaries on his poems almost line by line, thereby clarifying all that was obscure. His enemies, on the other hand, wrote copiously to criticize and oppose his poetic system. And the polemic on Góngora and gongorism or *culteranismo*, is the outstanding event in the history of our literary doctrines in the seventeenth century. His reputation as a poet even affected his personal life, as the following amusing anecdote indicates. Góngora applied for the position of Royal chaplain and was granted it by the King. But it appears that someone objected that such an obscure poet should not be named Royal Chaplain. To which a friend of Góngora's retorted: "Is there any law that requires royal chaplains to be fools?"

Góngora in his day, then, was accused of being unintelligible. Yet if we consider the matter more closely we see by the work of his commentators that he was perfectly understood. And he was imitated so much that his is the predominant influence on the lyric throughout the century. And yet his reputation for obscurity pursued him. He was divided into two personalities: the angel of light and the angel of darkness. Until our time he has been considered mainly as the angel of darkness. But today, ever since a group of intelligent scholars and poets, Dámaso Alonso, the most prominent among them, has tried to read Góngora's work closely, with the necessary effort, we know— leaving aside the consideration of whether he is or is not a great poet, appeals to some and not to others—that he is a perfectly intelligible poet. Intelligible, even clear, when he is followed along his road, along the path he traced for his poetry. For it is erroneous and absurd, in this case of "difficult poet" versus "public" to seek an approach to his poetry over routes other than those indicated by him. There is no mysterious poet without his key. Every mysterious poet, if he is a true poet, gives us, with his poetry, a key with which to decipher its mystery. So that it is senseless and dishonest to try to explain it by means foreign to its own way of being. You will admit that we should not think much of the ability or curiosity of an Englishman who in trying to penetrate the meaning of a German passage insisted on looking up the words in an Italian-English dictionary. Góngora needed his difficulty. He could not have created his poetry without it. Difficulty was no mere whim or eccentricity of his. It corresponded with his poetical way of being. Without it we should not have his magnificent poetry. And that is what always justifies difficulty or obscurity in an artist: its vital reason or need to be difficult in order to be; the need to be difficult or not be at all. In considering Góngora's attitude toward reality I shall try to show that his excellence and originality are inseparable from his difficulty; they are, in fact, one and the same thing.

I shall refer only to his most important work, the poem *Soledades*. It is an incomplete work of which we have only two parts, one and two. It seems to be, in general, a narrative poem. We are told that a young man, disdained by the woman he loves, arrives after we know not what adventures, at a coast clinging to a fragile board. Some goatherds give him lodging and he spends the night with them. On the following day he continues his journey and comes upon a group of peasants on their way to a rustic wedding. He joins them and attends the wedding which is celebrated with dances, fireworks and athletic contests until the bride and groom leave. And thus the first *Soledad* ends. In the second, the young man appears on a river-bank where he meets some fishermen and is invited home by them, all of which is told us in great detail. He watches the fishermen at work, explores the small barren island where they live and when, on the following day, his friends come to take him back to terra firma, he sees from the boat an animated falconry hunt with many hunters and great numbers of birds of chase. As you see, the story in itself is not much. But that is because the *Soledades* is not really a narrative poem. All that we have related is but a canvas on which the poet paints with marvelous fantasy all sorts of lyrical and descriptive caprices. The narrative part, the story is nothing but a slight pretext. Góngora makes use of it in order to indulge in descriptions of nature, plants, animals, landscape, in order to present dances, festivities, activities like hunting and fishing, all of the greatest variety. The development of the action is extremely slow and is constantly interrupted. The poet stops at any detail, takes delight in the most minute aspect of what his eyes see, then presents it with wonderful metaphors, in dazzling pictures full of color and movement. What can be deduced from all this? That the story of the *Soledades* is of slight import, that the important thing is the subject. And the subject is none other than the world, its external forms, its reality. In no other

Spanish poem does material reality, things, beings, animals, play such an essential and primary role. *Soledades* is a great poem of reality, of external reality, of sensual reality. Góngora was a sensual Andalusian to whom the world represented itself not in ideas or moral values but in volume, forms, seductive appearances.

Reality in the works of the poets that we have studied until now was merely a point of departure which they transcended to higher conceptions, or which they copied faithfully as in the Middle Ages. But for Góngora reality is the beginning and end of his poetry. How, then, can we explain that Góngora's poetry, if what I say is true, has appeared obscure and unintelligible? If it is poetry of the real, the logical thing would be that it should be perfectly clear to everybody. But that is not the case. Reality is indeed his subject-matter. But his poetry is not realistic. Reality does not mean realism until the nineteenth century when the realistic school proclaims that the only way to transcribe reality is to make a faithful human copy of it. Góngora's secret is that he does not reproduce reality as it appears before his eyes, in its normal lines and dimensions, but magnifies it, exalts it, as few poets have done. Why? Let us remember that reality for Góngora is his theme, his poetical object. But can reality as it is be a poetical object? Not for Góngora. A fundamental principle seems to underly his poetic conception which I might formulate thus: the poetic insufficiency of reality. Pure, crude reality is not sufficiently poetic, it never really has poetic character. Telling and describing what one sees is not poetry. What must be done to convert it into poetry? Raise it,

intensify its characteristics to an extreme degree, elevate it
above its natural forms and extract from the latter all their
esthetic content by means of the imagination and fantasy.
Reality must be transformed, transmuted into another kind
of poetic reality, material, sonorous, plastic, but not idealized; the artist must operate on it with the magic power of
word, metaphor, image. Let us consider some illustrations.

The young protagonist of the poem, shipwrecked, arrives at a coast clinging to a piece of timber:

> A pitying limb from mountain pine, opposed,
> The constant enemy to Notus' strife,
> Became no puny dolphin on that day
> To the unthinking traveller who reposed,
>
> *Del siempre en la montaña opuesto pino*
> *al enemigo Noto,*
> *piadoso miembro roto*
> *—breve tabla—delfín no fué pequeño*
> *al inconsiderado peregrino*

Notice the thematic word here, timber. That word in itself is not poetical. But Góngora converts the real and
humble timber into poetic timber by saying: A pine board,
pine, the tree on the mountain that resists the harshest
wind, the North wind, a board that was a limb broken off
from the boat on which he was sailing, a merciful board
because it took pity on the young man and let him cling to
it in order to be rescued, served him as a dolphin on whose
back he could come ashore. The method is very clear.
Around the words pine board, we see elaborated by the
association of poetic ideas, the visions of the tree on the
mountain, the desolating wind, first. Then that of the

shattered boat, of the feeling of pity inspired in one of its limbs by the youth. And finally the sea animal, the dolphin gracefully crossing the sea. What has Góngora done? Converted a poor sad object of material reality, timber, into a center of rich visions, mountain, wind, shipwreck, dolphin. Starting from the normal reality of the timber we arrive at superreality exaggerated and exalted. The fantasy operates on the real, draws, extracts from it a whole series of suggestions, evocations, that surround it with wealth and splendor, that raise it, in short, to an esthetic reality, to a poetic reality, from the simple level of material reality. That is the usual gongoristic method applied to everything in the visible world.

Here are more illustrations. On enumerating the presents brought by the peasants to the wedding feast, Góngora runs into hens. Some peasants bring a few of these domestic fowl in their hands:

> One bore a heavy burden in his hand
> Of pendant birds, the crested and the dun,
> Whose spouse, canorous herald to the sun,
> Wakeful although lascivious, has told
> The glories of his master to the land;
> Beaded with coral, on his head behold
> A turban bound with purple if not gold.

> *Cuál dellos las pendientes sumas graves*
> *de negras baja, de crestadas aves,*
> *cuyo lascivo esposo vigilante*
> *doméstico es del sol nuncio canoro,*
> *y—de coral barbado—no de oro*
> *ciñe, sino de púrpura, turbante.*

That is, Góngora finds himself before a bird, the hen, that has never been a favorite with poets. The dove, swan, gerfalcon, eagle were suitable poetic animals in the classical age. But not the hen, extremely simple and modest barnyard fowl, emblem of all that is prosaic, a bird that soars as little in poetry as in the air. What could he do with it? Góngora does not even name it. The word hen does not appear in the poem. But he says instead: crested birds whose lustful, vigilant husband, the cock, is the herald and announcer of the rising sun, who crows aloud, has a coral beard and wears besides, for greater splendor a purple turban. You see here the same gongoristic method: first he replaces the hen by her husband, the cock, who though not precisely an heroic animal has nevertheless at least more poetic attributes, grace, haughtiness, valor and is the king of the barnyard. By this simple substitution the hen is dignified much as some humble women are by their husbands' brilliance and fame. He presents the rooster, moreover, at his most seductive moment, from a plastic point of view, when he struts about at dawn and fills the air with his voice; he presents him in his crowing, that is, auditively. And then, pictorially, in the color of his beard and crest which he compares with a turban. How far Góngora has gone from the word hen! See what he has drawn from it, all that he has made us perceive: dawn, the rising of the sun in all the splendor of a new day, one of the most beautiful moments in Nature. The crowing of the cock, that awakens so many evocations in us, like the very voice of the country, when we are there and before our eyes perceive the light of day and we hear, half-asleep, its joyful trumpet. The idea of a herald, that is, of promise, the announcement of something that will happen, a happy on-coming event. And finally the word turban applied to the crest adds an exotic note, oriental, in its power of plastic evocation. Couldn't this be called a work of magic, a real alchemistic operation that transmutes the basest materials into the precious metal of poetry?

He does the same with trees as he does with the timber or hen. Take, for instance, some poplars along a river bank that are presented to us as fireworks on display. That is the reality. The poet does not name or describe the poplars. He says:

> Thereon the old man led him to the trees,
> Sacred to Hercules,
> Not far away, that braided their green hair,
> The stream their mirror and their light the glare

> *De Alcides le llevó luego a las plantas,*
> *que estaban, no muy lejos,*
> *trenzándose el cabello verde a cuantas*
> *da el fuego luces y el arroyo espejos.*

The plants of Alcides (referring to the myth according to which Phaëton's sisters mourned his death at the riverbank where he fell) are braiding their hair in the light of the fireworks and before the mirror of the waves. That is, Góngora makes over the myth, changes the plants into maidens and presents them as bending over the water, combing their hair in the mysterious light of the fireworks. Out of a few trees he draws a vision of incomparable charm, transforming them into a group of girls in graceful occupation and posture. And from the word poplar we get to mythology, Phaëton, shining mirrors, the reflection of colored lights in running water.

Let us take one final example, not of a thing, animal or tree, but an action. Some peasants go over the mountain to the place where the wedding is to be held. What is the reality? A number of people, so many dots on the landscape, walking across the fields. And Góngora offers us this comparison: they are like a flock of cranes that cross seas of air, not like flying boats but like birds with sails full of wind, scattered over the azure, tracing designs that sometimes look like the waxing moon, others like the waning moon, or perhaps better still like mysterious words written with feathers in flight across the diaphanous paper of the heavens:

> Thereon all passed, arranged the company,
> As at the Equinox we furrowing see
>   The high seas of the air
>   No flying galleys' hulls
>   But the swift-sailing gulls,
> Sometimes like moons that either wax or wane
> Distant the extremes of their band they bear,
> At other times winged characters they feign
> Upon the sky diaphanous to write
> As parchment, for the feathers of their flight.

> *Pasaron todos pues, y regulados*
> *cual en los equinocios surcar vemos*
> *los piélagos del aire libre algunas*
> *volantes no galeras,*
> *sino grullas veleras,*
> *tal vez creciendo, tal menguando lunas*
> *sus distantes extremos,*
> *caracteres tal vez formando alados*
> *en el papel diáfano del cielo*
> *las plumas de su vuelo.*

I don't think that there is to be found in Castilian poetry a sustained metaphor of greater beauty or elegance. It has all the charm and exquisiteness of a Japanese print. Góngora has converted the place of the scene, ground, earth, into sky but at the same time into sea, by comparing the cranes with celestial barks. And he has associated their movement with the forms of the moon. But the metaphor is crowned with that image of celestial writing in which the sky is compared with delicate and transparent paper.

I think that now we shall be in a position to understand two things much better. One, the beauty of Góngora's poetry, the innumerable elements of plastic fantasy, of imaginative reality. Another, its difficulty, the reason for its difficulty. And what is this? His method of treating reality. In all the illustrations cited, reality is but a slight thematic prop. The timber, hen, poplars, group of peasants are a mere point of departure. But since they in themselves are not poetry and Góngora wishes to create poetry he has no choice but to unmake them, as it were. The real objects are completely submerged in the sea of metaphors and images that they inspire in the poet. In this game of substitutions, Góngora goes further and further from his material foundation, from his real theme, and so rises above the real that the real is forgotten, is lost sight of. It is difficult to see a hen behind that interposition of images. And the result could not be more paradoxical. Reality, by dint of being exalted, raised to esthetic value, disappears, is pulverized, is lost. Góngora who loves reality so much and loves to see its beautiful things, suppresses it, destroys it. To what end? In order to give us another reality, poetically created with true reality.

And so we can understand why many people who demand that things be called by their names, that they be nothing more than they appear, see nothing in this poetry, are indeed incapable of seeing anything in it. A great master of Spanish criticism, Menéndez y Pelayo, actually said that *Soledades* is a nihilistic poem, that it represents poetic nihilism or nothingness. When, as a matter of fact, they represent plenitude; nowhere in the Spanish lyric are there present realities more rich and dense. This poetry might be called good or bad according to one's individual judgment. But what cannot legitimately be said is that it is empty, that it is nothingness. To be sure, it requires a much greater intellectual effort and quickness of perception than the reading of a newspaper. Góngora is no poet of the normal. But he starts from the normal. He is a poet of reality but not a realistic poet. There is a Spanish proverb that says, advising simple and direct language: " Bread, bread and wine, wine " or as you say "Call a spade a spade." Góngora would never call bread, bread or wine, wine. His poetic system is the opposite of this. Why? In all material reality, in the form of things, there is infinite potentiality. If things are seen as they are, they end at once, they are said in a moment. And reality in itself is a mere catalogue of things. Góngora is enamoured of the real. But he exalts it, ennobles it in such a way that the world becomes a marvelous feast for the imagination and the senses. That is his attitude. He does not analyze, reproduce, doubt reality, nor does he humbly accept it. His is poetry of pride; poetry of exaltation and adventure. Góngora, like a good Spaniard, is passionate. He has a passion for the substance of material reality. He looks at the world with eyes of sensual love. We spoke earlier of the mystical poets and said that the mystic exalts the powers of the spirit, its capacity to penetrate the mystery. And Góngora exalts the powers of matter. And in that sense, he is a mystic too, he is the mystic of material reality, unequalled in Spanish poetry to this day.

VI

THE REVOLT AGAINST REALITY

José de Espronceda

VI

Góngora is the last poet of the classical period. After his death, for almost two centuries it may be said that there is no great poetry in Spain. Only after the romantic revolution could another great poetic personality appear. But by then the world had taken one of its strides toward new horizons. And the world we shall see now is nothing like the world we have seen. And why? Because our instrument for perceiving, feeling, interpreting the world, man, is completely changed. By the beginning of the nineteenth century a new type of man treads the earth. Mountains remain in their places, rivers run their course, seasons follow one another in usual order. But the eyes that see them, the conscience that questions them, the mind that tries to give meaning to these appearances are new. And the object of sight, what the eyes see is changed and transformed by the mere fact that the glance and soul that contemplate it are changed. Reality will be different because man is different. And it is in this romantic period that the constant conflict between the real and the poetic worlds arrives at its climax, that the combat between external and internal reality takes its most violent forms and ends most tragically. I shall speak of the poet in Spain who best represents that new man and his attitude toward the world.

His name was José de Espronceda and his life is a perfect compendium of romantic lives. It seems as though uncertainty awaited him from his very birth, for he was not born at home but outdoors, on a trip his mother was taking. The tonic note of his life, as in the case of all romantics, was disconformity. He was educated in the classical tradition by a teacher who was the last representative of the old literary school. But from that classical education he drew only a sense of revolt against the classical, and a vehement desire to destroy it. At fifteen his adventures begin. Spain was at that time agitated by political strife between partisans of absolute and constitutional monarchy, that is, the absolutists and liberals. Espronceda was an ardent liberal and organized with some other boys, during the period of absolutist tyranny, a secret society dedicated to conspiracy against the régime. They used to meet in the cellar of a pharmacy illuminated with red lanterns and they wore black gowns and masks. Nothing but children's play? Of course, that group of boys can hardly be taken seriously, but in the way they chose to play one can see already something of that restlessness of Espronceda's, that impulse toward revolt which was the axis of his soul. They were found out but because they were mere children the punishment was light. Espronceda continues his studies but, hungry for adventure, he decides, at eighteen, to explore the world on his own, and embarks at Gibraltar for Lisbon. Here is an amusing detail: on approaching Lisbon, as he admired the magnificence of the bay in the Tagus and the beauty of the city, Espronceda counted his worldly wealth. He has two pesetas. He throws them into the sea, the story goes, so that he will not enter such a great city with so little money. The symbol of a man who throws himself into life alone, with nothing more than his own vital force to spur him on.

In Lisbon, according to his early biographers, in London, according to later ones, he meets the woman who is to be the center of his sentimental life. She is Teresa, the daughter of a political émigré. He falls in love with the girl, violently, of course, for a romantic cannot fall in love otherwise. But the poet's beloved does what so many poets' loves have done: she makes a marriage of convenience with a rich merchant. That, however, is no obstacle for romantic love and is of easy solution: the poet resorts to abduction. He carries Teresa off, later, in Paris. He had fought in the July Revolution and had taken part in an attempt of a daring group of liberals to enter Spain. The love of Espronceda and Teresa is agitated and turbulent. They go to Madrid together but their differences are intensified and Teresa abandons him. He searches for her, they come together again, but soon after, she flees again definitively. And they will never see each other again alive. We do not know how Teresa spent the last years of her life but we do know that Espronceda managed to see her dead through the window of the room where her corpse lay. This sentimental adventure fixes an indelible stamp on Espronceda's life, a stamp that no romantic's live could be without: an unhappy love, a passion with a tragic end.

Espronceda continues his career as writer and politician, his social ideas ever more radical. He begins to publish his poems, takes part in all the revolutions and, on the triumph of the liberals, is given a diplomatic post at the Hague and is elected deputy. Life seems to be opening a smoother course for him. He thinks of marrying. But at this moment death overtakes him, at the age of 34. And so he receives his final consecration as romantic: premature death. What can we conclude from the rapid review of these facts? Three essential data: his passionate, stormy love opposed and vanquished by life. His life of constant struggle, of open revolt against almost all that surrounded him. And his end before his time, the brutal coming of death, that romantic death that delighted in cutting off the destinies of so many great poets, Byron, Shelley, Keats, Leopardi, Espronceda. That romantic death that was perhaps really a happy stroke of destiny, for although it may seem to us biologically premature, it was perhaps the best and most fitting solution for those violent lives that burnt themselves out like flames, that had, perhaps, to last fewer years since they were lived with maximum intensity, since they gave all they had with a vital generosity that exhausted them.

What is reality or the world for this romantic man? In the first place, a mystery. A mystery whose key lies in the hands of a superior being, God, toward whom man turns in an attitude of questioning, of challenge. That conception of the world as mystery is one of the most powerful impulses of the romantic soul. We find anxiety over the unknown in several of Espronceda's works, but I should like to show it to you in one that adopts a legendary theme and has as its protagonist a legendary being as well. Spanish romanticism is predominantly historical-minded and disinters many epic themes of the past, creating a new legendary poetry. Espronceda, though much less affected by this tendency to external and historical romanticism than other Spanish romantics, did not escape its influence completely however. And he treated in his *Estudiante de Salamanca* a traditional subject, no ordinary traditional subject, but the story of the great Spanish gentleman Don Juan who was created by Tirso de Molina at the beginning of the seventeenth century and was to take so many different forms in all literature ever since. Espronceda, then, takes his hero and the theme of his poem from the past. Don Félix de Montemar is a violent, irreligious, insolent young man who fears nothing and trusts only in his sword and valor. His life is spent in love and gambling, never looking back or ahead, challenging men and courting women. Among his victims is the lovely Elvira. Don Félix seduces her and abandons her and she dies heartbroken. But the gentleman does not even remember her. We see him in a gambling scene, cynical and disillusioned, staking all on his cards. At this moment the brother of the seduced and abandoned Elvira appears and demands reparation of Don Félix for his dishonor. The libertine Don Juan kills him too.

Until now the legend has unfolded on a traditional plane, with nothing new added. But from this moment on, the romantic vision takes more and more complete possession of the poem. Don Félix, his sword in his hand, having just killed the brother of the betrayed Elvira, walks along the narrow street where the duel has taken place. He suddenly hears a mysterious sigh at his side. It is a strange white form, the form of a woman in a white dress who is kneeling before an image placed in a vaulted niche, on the street, and who then stands up and begins to walk. So strange is her appearance that Don Félix is at first terrified. But the soul of the seducer Don Juan soon recovers: it is a woman, a mysterious woman, alone on a solitary street on a dark night. No Don Juan can hesitate: his blood, his destiny as lover orders him to follow her, discover her, conquer her. And then one of the most fascinating pursuits imaginable takes place. The woman shadow slips quietly along the streets, so mysterious that at times she might be taken for a ray of moonlight or foam on the sea. The gentleman speaks to her, asks her anxiously who she is, over and over again, but without securing an answer. But that does not abate his boldness. He tells the mute lady in haughty words that he must know who she is, where she is going and that he will follow her in spite of everything. " Though it be to hell, though heaven try to prevent it," says Don Félix, "my desire to know who you are shall be fulfilled." This is a new turn to the legend. Don Juan, the traditional Don Juan, was a libertine, seducer of women, possessed by inexhaustible sensual love. But what impels this new descendent of his in Espronceda's poem? Actually, he has found the form of a woman one night, pursues it, but as the pursuit continues we become aware that the woman ceases to be a mere sensual attraction for the seducer, but gradually is converted into something more disquieting and strange: into a mystery. Don Félix no longer pursues a woman, but a mystery, an enigmatic, unknown being. And the words we quoted are very significant. He wishes to know who she is, where she is bound. Impelled by his ardent desire, he will follow her against heaven and hell. His desire? This word, the basic word of romanticism, what does it mean here? Is it Don Juan's desire a sensual desire? No it is the romantic longing of the soul as it faces the world and its mystery, the desire to decipher the enigma of reality. And that amorous adventure, so charged with symbolic content, continues along the narrow winding streets of the old city. Finally the lady speaks. She tells the gentleman not to persist in following her, for great risk is involved, and that his last hour may be approaching without his knowing it. But the seducer answers that he will not give up his desire for anything in the world. It does not matter if it costs him his life. And he continues behind her. Suddenly a strange, illuminated suite is seen on the street and funereal chants are intoned. It is a funeral procession. Don Félix asks who is dead and one of the mourners informs him that it is he himself. Don Félix shudders with terror, but soon regains his calm and bursts out laughing. The woman speaks again and warns her pursuer that with each step he takes he is approaching his death. But Don Félix does not withdraw this time either. " Life has but one end, the soul has but one halting-place," he answers. " Onward." The lady stops before a door through which they enter into some fantastic galleries, quiet and deserted, and along which they vaguely see strange spectral figures. The whole description leaves an impression of strangeness, terror, mystery, hallucination.

And yet it is at this moment that the figure of Don Félix seems most gigantic and grandiose to us. Now we realize his complete transformation. What is this man, mocker of women, professional lover? A great deal more. The poet says: he is a soul in revolt whom fear can never deter. He is a fragile fabric made of impure matter, to be sure, but within him a generous spirit breathes that does not accept the prison of life, that rises before God trying to equal him, and asking him to yield the secret of his immensity. Now we realize that the traditional character Don Juan has lost all the geographical and historical attributes that made him a hero in the seventeenth century and that he is simply the new man, romantic man, who rises against the mystery of life and reality and faces God with an attitude of satanical rebellion. It is the man who will not resign himself to his own limits, to not knowing and that is why this man follows the mysterious lady to the end. And the end of Espronceda's legend is death. That lady was none other than death and in the final scene Don Félix celebrates his macabre marriage with death itself. How can this be interpreted? After the anxious pursuit, man rebellious and tormented, finds no other solution for the enigma of life than another enigma, death. Reality, the universe, life do not yield their mystery, no matter how much one pursues them. Or the key to this mystery is simply death. But death is final, the absolute end of life, and not a passage to a higher and eternal life. It is the death of the romantic in open revolt, in despair, the terrible death without future life. This attitude that we find in Espronceda's legendary poem can be seen even more clearly in his lyric.

If we consider his poems, especially the *Canto a Teresa*, the elegy he wrote to the woman who was the great love of his life, we can trace with greater precision the poet's attitude toward reality. How does the poet regard the real world? Espronceda passes through three stages. The first is an ardent love of reality. The poet feels an attraction for everything, likes everything, finds that life offers him an inexhaustible repertory of temptations and beauties. I might call this stage his entrance into the world, his initiation in life. Espronceda expresses it with two kinds of metaphors: one is a ship:

> This life of mine seemed in those happy days
> Like some tall vessel, that in all her pride
> First leaves the port, and her gay flag displays

> *Mi vida entonces, cual guerrera nave*
> *Que el puerto deja por la vez primera,*
> *Y al soplo de los céfiros suave,*
> *Orgullosa despliega su bandera.*

The other metaphor is the comet:

> Flung as a rapid comet wide,
> On ardent fancy's wing I flew,
> Where'er my wayward mind spied
> Or joys, or triumphs to pursue.

> *Yo me lancé cual rápido cometa*
> *En alas de mi ardiente fantasía.*
> *Doquier mi arrebatada mente inquieta*
> *Dichas y triunfos encontrar creía.*

Both metaphors give the same impression of an impulse onward, of a magnificent impelling force. That is the first stage of the romantic feeling toward life. " I loved everything," Espronceda says. A vehement love of everything, a burning desire to embrace all the beauties of the world. As in the *Estudiante de Salamanca,* the protagonist is a lover who rushes furiously after the form through which he catches a glimpse of the mystery of reality. In short, in his initial attitude toward reality the romantic is an ardent lover who throws himself into the sea or sky of the world, mad with desire and longing. He believes that in the real world which his eyes see, gilded by the morning light of youth, is to be found what he desires with infinite longing.

For a moment the poet loves the world and has endless hope in it. But then the contact is made. Man approaches reality and demands that it give him all that he expected to find in it: love, beauty, glory, virtue. And as he compares the dreams of his soul, that is, the contents of his inner world, of his poetic world, with the forms of the outer real world, his faith and enthusiasm diminish with vertiginous rapidity. What does the poet find in that heaven into which he threw himself? Espronceda tells us that he finds nothing but doubt, that celestial beauty has become an illusion of air. And the earth? He has anxiously, deliriously sought, he says, glory, goodness. And he has found nothing but fetid dust, wretched dross:

> Then on the earth I anxious sought
> For virtue, glory, love sublime;
> And my worn spirit found there nought
> But fetid dust and loathsome slime.

> *Luego en la tierra, la virtud, la gloria*
> *busqué con ansia y delirante amor;*
> *y hediondo polvo y deleznable escoria*
> *mi fatigado espíritu encontró.*

As for love, he had dreamed of women of virginal purity enveloped in white clouds. But as soon as one comes near them, the purity changes into mire and corruption. This is the second stage in the romantic attitude toward the world of reality: disenchantment, bitter disillusionment, without remedy.

As the romantic advances through real life illuminated and enkindled by his inner world, he leaves behind him bits of hope, illusion and life at each one of the stages along the way. Reality can produce nothing of what the inner life has forged. "Desire is," says Espronceda, "eternal and insatiable." Here lies the difference between his attitude and that of the moralist like Manrique whom we discussed in the second lecture. There, too, real life was pronounced empty and unsatisfactory but only in comparison with eternal life. Here in romanticism it is very different. That basis of comparing reality with something higher, with something to be attained by contemplating the beyond, has been lost. The romantic compares everything with his desire, with his longing and nothing more. So that if life cannot satisfy this longing he has no hope left. He does not resign himself like the Christian poet, he does not determine to live valiantly the dream of the world, if it is nothing but a dream. Even rebellious, he rises satanically against unsatisfactory life and curses it. Here is a definitive line of Espronceda's:

> I felt the real, and I hated life,
> And peace believed but in the grave.
>
> *Palpé la realidad y odié la vida.*
> *Sólo en la paz de los sepulcros creo.*

That is, his poetic world tried, touched the real world, and from this contact drew only hatred and malediction. What solution can be left? Resignation? No. This modern man has no faith, his moral springs are broken. Escape? Also impossible. He is a rebel who never abandons the struggle at any cost, just as Don Félix never gave up the pursuit of the lady. There is no other way out but death. After the line quoted the poet adds: I believe only in the peace of the grave. This is the third and final stage in the romantic attitude: despair, hatred, death while rebelling. Man has no choice but to die or to go on living only externally. He could go on like a living corpse, Espronceda tells us at the end of the *Canto a Teresa,* with his heart shattered, pretending by external acts to be alive, but with his soul completely destroyed. That irreducible, invincible opposition between the poetic and the real world is expressed in the final stanza of the poem in an extremely sarcastic and cruel manner. Everything in the external world is beautiful: the crystalline sphere shines with dazzling light; spring heightens the beauty of the fields. Cruel reality disdains the suffering of man. And he writes his famous stanza:

> Be glad while yet ye may! The crystal sphere
> Revolves in golden light, and life is fair.
> Whoever yet could stay in her career
> The Earth, that bids rejoice? See, in mid air
> The radiant sunbeams dance! See, year by year
> The fields and forests their Spring vesture wear!
> Let then deep-seated sorrow change to mirth;
> Who recks of one more corpse laid low in earth?

Gocemos, sí; la cristalina esfera
Gira bañada en luz: ¡bella es la vida!
¿Quién a parar alcanza la carrera
Del mundo hermoso que al placer convida?
Brilla radiante el sol, la primavera
Los campos pinta en la estación florida:
Truéquese en risa mi dolor profundo.
Que haya un cadáver más¿qué importa al mundo?

Here we see the desperate complaint against the indifference, the brutality of reality. We see here man who feels himself irreparably sundered from it. They cannot get along. The earth turns joyfully round while he feels his heart destroyed. It is a solution without a solution. In Garcilasso, in Manrique, in Góngora, in one way or another, that difference between the real and the poetic world was indeed evident but it was somehow resolved. By accepting it or idealizing it or by fleeing from it. But not in the romantic. That is why this act of the drama that I have endeavored to unfold before you, that of the conflicts between the real and poetic worlds, is the most tragic and desolating of all. There is no possible arrangement or agreement. Reality is odious when one sees it close to. And the two worlds remain thus, opposing each other like enemies.

At the end of the first lecture we spoke of the paradisaical period of man: unity. Unity of reality and the inner world. Now we must use the word that expresses the extreme opposite: division. Modern man, this new man, is man divided, in the highest degree. And he will continue to live desperately in a world which is his because he is born into it, but which is not his, since he cannot adapt it to what he feels within him. The two worlds are not only different but even hostile. The real world destroys the poetic world and denies it all possibility of expression. And the only grandeur that poetry still retains at this stage of the human spirit is the grandeur of the complaint, the desperate cry, the magnificent revolt of the poetic world, of human illusion, against the real world.

I have tried to show how Spanish poetry, through the ages, has found for that insuperable problem of the two worlds, the poetic and the real, a series of solutions, each more beautiful than the other. Many people used to, and still do, look upon the writing of poetry as a capricious and inconsequential pastime, the amusement of a few beings, who withdraw from life and cast luminous words into the air. But if one contemplates the poet's work with any seriousness—poetic seriousness, I mean—it becomes evident that, far from remaining pleasantly outside the world, he lives at its very center.

A few years ago, Garcilasso was considered a poet of elegance and refinement, but no one felt in his poetry the wonderful vibration of his struggle with the other world. Until recently, Góngora was thought to be only a poet of surfaces, one who glided over reality with dazzling brilliance but with supreme indifference; no one realized the fierce battle he fought with ordinary, existing reality for the sake of an imaginative, created reality. In these lectures, I have tried to show, over and above differences of period and style, of temperament and theme, the great profundity of spiritual effort which goes into the making of those perfect forms, apparently so light; the great intensity of thought that the true poet applies to his prodigious circensian game of leaping from trapeze to trapeze, from world to world, through the widest spaces.